PYTHON PROGRAMMING SERIES 2

THIS BOOK INCLUDES:

"PYTHON FOR BEGINNERS +PYTHON PROGRAMMING + LEARN PYTHON PROGRAMMING"

BY JOHN BROWN

PYTHON FOR BEGINNERS

CHAPTER 1. INTRODUCTION TO PYTHON 14

1.1 WHY DO PEOPLE USE PYTHON? 14

1.1.1 PYTHON IS POPULAR 16

1.1.2 SOFTWARE QUALITY 17

1.1.3 DEVELOPER PRODUCTIVITY 18

1.2 IS PYTHON A "SCRIPTING LANGUAGE"? 19

1.3 BUT WHAT'S THE DOWNSIDE? 20

1.4 WHO USES PYTHON TODAY? 21

1.5 WHAT CAN I DO WITH PYTHON? 24

1.5.1 SYSTEMS PROGRAMMING 25

1.5.2 GUIS 25

1.5.3 INTERNET SCRIPTING 26

1.5.4 COMPONENT INTEGRATION 27

1.5.5 DATABASE PROGRAMMING 28

1.5.6 RAPID PROTOTYPING 28

1.5.7 NUMERIC AND SCIENTIFIC PROGRAMMING 29

1.5.8 GAMING, IMAGES, SERIAL PORTS, XML, ROBOTS, AND MORE . 29

1.6 HOW IS PYTHON SUPPORTED? 30

1.7 WHAT ARE PYTHON'S TECHNICAL STRENGTHS? 31

1.7.1 IT'S OBJECT-ORIENTED 31

1.7.2 IT'S FREE 31

1.7.3 IT IS PORTABLE 33

1.7.4 IT IS POWERFUL 34

1.7.5 IT IS MIXABLE 35

1.7.6 IT IS EASY TO USE 36

1.7.7 IT IS EASY TO LEARN 36

1.7.8 IT IS NAMED AFTER MONTY PYTHON 36

1.8 HOW DOES PYTHON STACK UP TO LANGUAGE X?........................ 38

1.9 CHAPTER SUMMARY 40

1.10 PYTHON IS ENGINEERING, NOT ART 40

CHAPTER 2. HOW PYTHON RUNS PROGRAMS 44

2.1 INTRODUCING THE PYTHON INTERPRETER............................ 44

2.2 PROGRAM EXECUTION 47

2.2.1 THE PROGRAMMER'S VIEW 47

2.2.2 PYTHON'S VIEW 48

2.3 EXECUTION MODEL VARIATIONS 52

2.3.1 PYTHON IMPLEMENTATION ALTERNATIVES 52

2.3.2 EXECUTION OPTIMIZATION TOOLS 55

2.3.3 FROZEN BINARIES 58

2.3.4 OTHER EXECUTION OPTIONS 60

2.3.5 FUTURE POSSIBILITIES? 61

CHAPTER 3. HOW YOU 63

3.1 THE INTERACTIVE PROMPT 64

3.1.1 RUNNING CODE INTERACTIVELY 65

3.1.2 WHY THE INTERACTIVE PROMPT? 67

3.1.3 USING THE INTERACTIVE PROMPT 69

3.2 SYSTEM COMMAND LINES AND FILES 72

3.2.1 A FIRST SCRIPT 73

CONCLUSION 76

PYTHON PROGRAMMING

CHAPTER 1. RUNNING FILES WITH COMMAND LINES IN PYTHON 81

1.1 USING COMMAND LINES AND FILES 82

1.2 UNIX EXECUTABLE SCRIPTS 84

1.3 CLICKING FILE ICONS 86

1.3.1 CLICKING ICONS ON WINDOWS 86

1.3.2 THE INPUT TRICK 88

1.3.3 OTHER ICON CLICK LIMITATIONS 89

1.4 MODULE IMPORTS AND RELOADS 91

1.4.1 THE GRANDER MODULE STORY: ATTRIBUTES 94

1.4.2 IMPORT AND RELOAD USAGE NOTES 98

1.5 USING EXEC TO RUN MODULE FILES 99

1.6 THE IDLE USER INTERFACE 100

1.6.1 IDLE BASICS 101

1.6.2 USING IDLE 104

1.6.3 ADVANCED IDLE TOOLS 107

1.7 OTHER IDES 108

1.8 OTHER LAUNCH OPTIONS 110

1.8.1 EMBEDDING CALLS 110

1.8.2 FROZEN BINARY EXECUTABLE 111

1.8.3 TEXT EDITOR LAUNCH OPTIONS 112

1.8.4 STILL OTHER LAUNCH OPTIONS 112

1.8.5 FUTURE POSSIBILITIES? 113

1.9 WHICH OPTION SHOULD I USE? 113

1.10 DEBUGGING PYTHON CODE 114

CHAPTER 2. INTRODUCING PYTHON OBJECT TYPES 117

2.1 WHY USE BUILT IN TYPES? 118

2.1.1 PYTHON'S CORE DATA TYPES 119

2.2 NUMBERS 121
2.3 STRINGS 122
2.3.1 SEQUENCE OPERATIONS 123
2.3.2 IMMUTABILITY 124
2.3.3 TYPE SPECIFIC METHODS 125
2.3.4 GETTING HELP 126
2.3.5 OTHER WAYS TO CODE STRINGS 127
2.3.6 PATTERN MATCHING 128
2.4 LISTS 128
2.4.1 SEQUENCE OPERATIONS 128
2.4.2 TYPE SPECIFIC OPERATIONS 129
2.4.3 BOUNDS CHECKING 129
2.4.4 NESTING 130
2.4.5 COMPREHENSIONS 130
2.5 DICTIONARIES 132
2.5.1 MAPPING OPERATIONS 132
2.5.2 NESTING REVISITED 133
2.5.3 SORTING KEYS: FOR LOOPS 134
2.5.4 ITERATION AND OPTIMIZATION 136
2.5.5 MISSING KEYS: IF TESTS 137
2.6 TUPLES 138
2.6.1 WHY TUPLES? 138
2.7 FILES 138
2.7.1 OTHER FILE LIKE TOOLS 141
2.8 OTHER CORE TYPES 141
2.8.1 HOW TO BREAK YOUR CODE'S FLEXIBILITY 142
CONCLUSION 144

LEARN PYTHON PROGRAMMING

CHAPTER 1. INTRODUCTION TO NUMERIC TYPES IN PYTHON 149

1.1 NUMERIC TYPE BASICS 149

1.1.1 NUMERIC LITERALS 151

1.1.2 BUILT IN NUMERIC TOOLS 153

1.1.3 PYTHON EXPRESSION OPERATORS 153

1.2 NUMBERS IN ACTION 156

1.2.1 VARIABLES AND BASIC EXPRESSIONS 157

1.2.2 NUMERIC DISPLAY FORMATS 158

1.2.3 COMPARISONS: NORMAL AND CHAINED 159

1.2.4 DIVISION: CLASSIC, FLOOR, AND TRUE 160

1.2.5 INTEGER PRECISION 162

1.2.6 COMPLEX NUMBERS 163

1.2.7 HEXADECIMAL, OCTAL, AND BINARY NOTATION 163

1.2.8 BITWISE OPERATIONS 164

1.2.9 OTHER BUILT IN NUMERIC TOOLS 165

1.3 OTHER NUMERIC TYPES 166

1.3.1 DECIMAL TYPE 166

1.3.2 FRACTION TYPE 167

1.3.3 SETS 169

1.3.4 BOOLEANS 173

1.4 NUMERIC EXTENSIONS 175

CHAPTER 2. THE DYNAMIC TYPING INTERLUDE 176

2.1 THE CASE OF THE MISSING DECLARATION STATEMENTS 177

2.1.1 VARIABLES, OBJECTS, AND REFERENCES 177

2.1.2 TYPES LIVE WITH OBJECTS, NOT VARIABLES 180

2.1.3 OBJECTS ARE GARBAGE COLLECTED 181

2.2 SHARED REFERENCES 182

2.2.1 SHARED REFERENCES AND IN PLACE CHANGES 185

2.2.2 SHARED REFERENCES AND EQUALITY 187

2.3 DYNAMIC TYPING IS EVERYWHERE 188

CHAPTER 3. STRINGS 190

3.1 STRING LITERALS 192

3.1.1 SINGLE AND DOUBLE QUOTED STRINGS ARE THE SAME 192

3.1.2 ESCAPE SEQUENCES REPRESENT SPECIAL BYTES 192

3.1.3 RAW STRINGS SUPPRESS ESCAPES 194

3.1.4 TRIPLE QUOTES CODE MULTILINE BLOCK STRINGS 196

3.2 STRINGS IN ACTION 197

3.2.1 BASIC OPERATIONS 197

3.2.2 INDEXING AND SLICING 198

3.2.3 STRING CONVERSION TOOLS 202

3.2.4 CHANGING STRINGS 205

3.3 STRING METHODS 207

CONCLUSION 210

PYTHON FOR BEGINNERS

THE BEGINNERS GUIDE TO PYTHON PROGRAMMING STEP-BY-STEP

BY JOHN BROWN

© **Copyright 2021 by - All rights reserved.**

This document is geared towards providing exact and reliable information in regards to the topic and issue covered. The publication is sold with the idea that the publisher is not required to render accounting, officially permitted, or otherwise, qualified services. If advice is necessary, legal or professional, a practiced individual in the profession should be ordered.

- From a Declaration of Principles which was accepted and approved equally by a Committee of the American Bar Association and a Committee of Publishers and Associations.

In no way is it legal to reproduce, duplicate, or transmit any part of this document in either electronic means or in printed format. Recording of this publication is strictly prohibited and any storage of this document is not allowed unless with written permission from the publisher. All rights reserved.

The information provided herein is stated to be truthful and consistent, in that any liability, in terms of inattention or otherwise, by any usage or abuse of any policies, processes, or directions contained within is the solitary and utter responsibility of the recipient reader. Under no circumstances will any legal responsibility or blame be held against the publisher for any reparation, damages, or monetary loss due to the information herein, either directly or indirectly.

Respective authors own all copyrights not held by the publisher.

The information herein is offered for informational purposes solely and is universal as such. The presentation of the information is without a contract or any type of guarantee assurance.

The trademarks that are used are without any consent, and the publication of the trademark is without permission or backing by the trademark owner. All trademarks and brands within this book are for clarifying purposes only and are owned by the owners themselves, not affiliated with this document.

Chapter 1. Introduction to Python

On the off chance that you've purchased this book, you may definitely understand what Python is and why it's a significant apparatus to learn. In the event that you don't, you presumably will not be sold on Python until you've taken in the language by perusing the remainder of this book and have done a venture or two.

In any case, before we hop into subtleties, the initial not many pages of this book will momentarily present a portion of the principle purposes for Python's prominence. To start chiseling a definition of Python, this part appears as an inquiry and-answer meeting, which represents probably the most widely recognized inquiries posed by fledglings.

1.1 Why Do People Use Python?

Since there are many programming dialects accessible today, this is the typical first inquiry of newbies. Given that there are about 1 million Python clients out there right now, there truly is no real way to address this inquiry with complete exactness; the decision of advancement apparatuses is some of the time dependent on interesting limitations or individual inclination.

Yet, in the wake of instructing Python to around 225 gatherings and more than 3,000 understudies during the most recent 12 years, some basic subjects have arisen. The essential variables referred to by Python clients appear to be these:

Software quality: For some, Python's emphasis on lucidness, cognizance, and programming quality when all is said in done separates it from different instruments in the scripting scene. Python code is intended to be intelligible, and consequently reusable and viable substantially more so than conventional scripting dialects. The consistency of Python code makes it straightforward, regardless of whether you didn't compose it. Furthermore, Python has profound help for further developed programming reuse instruments, for example, object-situated programming (OOP).

Developer productivity: Python helps designer profitability ordinarily past arranged or statically composed dialects like C, C++, and Java. Python code is regularly 33% to one fifth the size of identical C++ or Java code. That implies there is less to type, less to troubleshoot, and less to keep up sometime later. Python programs additionally run quickly, without the protracted arrange and connection steps needed by some different apparatuses, further boosting developer speed.

Program portability: Most Python programs run unaltered on all significant PC stages. Porting Python code among Linux and Windows, for instance, is normally simply an issue of replicating a content's code between machines. In addition, Python offers various alternatives for coding versatile graphical UIs, information base access programs, electronic frameworks, and that's only the tip of the iceberg. In any event, working framework interfaces, including program dispatches and registry preparing, are as convenient in Python as they can be.

Support libraries: Python accompanies an enormous assortment of prebuilt and convenient usefulness, known as the standard library. This library upholds a variety of utilization level programming undertakings, from text design coordinating to arrange scripting. Moreover, Python can be reached out with both local libraries and a tremendous assortment of outsider application support programming. Python's outsider area offers apparatuses for site development, numeric programming, sequential port access, game turn of events, and considerably more. The NumPy expansion, for example, has been depicted as a free and all the more remarkable comparable to the Matlab numeric programming framework.

Component integration: Python contents can undoubtedly speak with different pieces of an application, utilizing an assortment of combination systems. Such mixes permit Python to be utilized as an item customization and expansion device. Today, Python code can conjure C and C++ libraries, can be called from C and C++ programs, can coordinate with Java furthermore, .NET segments, can convey over systems like COM, can interface with gadgets over sequential ports, and can cooperate over networks with interfaces like SOAP, XML-RPC, and CORBA. It's anything but an independent instrument.

Enjoyment: Due to Python's usability and inherent toolset, it can make the demonstration of programming more joy than task. Albeit this might be an elusive advantage, its impact on profitability is a significant resource.

Of these components, the initial two (quality and profitability) are presumably the most convincing advantages to most Python clients.

1.1.1 Python Is Popular

You may have heard that Python is mainstream. It might appear to be that it doesn't actually matter how famous a language is inasmuch as you can fabricate the application you need to work with it.

Yet, regardless, the fame of a programming language is a solid marker of the nature of libraries you'll have accessible to the quantity of employment opportunities you'll discover. So, you should will in general incline toward more mainstream advances as there will be more decisions and mixes accessible.

Anyway, is Python really that mainstream? Indeed it is. You'll discover a ton of promotion and exaggeration, however there are a lot of details backing this case. We should take a gander at some examination introduced by stackoverflow.com, a famous inquiry and-answer site for developers.

Stack Overflow runs a site called Stack Overflow Trends where you can take a gander at the patterns for different innovations by tag. At the point when you analyze. Python to the next likely up-and-comers you could pick to get the hang of programming, you'll see one is not normal for the others.

Notice the extraordinary development of Python contrasted with the level or even descending pattern of the other regular applicants! In case you're wagering your future on the accomplishment of a given innovation, which one would you browse this rundown?

That is only one diagram what does it truly advise us? Indeed, we should take a gander at another. Stack Overflow does a yearly overview of designers. It's extensive and done.

From that review, I'd prefer to point out you're a part named "Generally Loved, Dreaded, and Wanted Languages." In the "Most Wanted" segment, you'll discover information on the portion of "designers who are not creating with the language or innovation however have communicated interest in creating with it."

On the off chance that you concur with me that the overall ubiquity of a programming language matters, at that point Python is obviously a decent decision. Once more, in the diagram beneath, you'll see that Python is beating out everyone else and is well above even second spot:

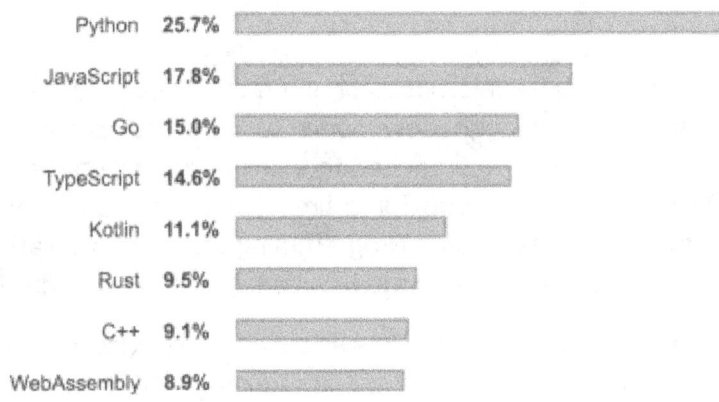

1.1.2 Software Quality

By plan, Python carries out a purposely basic and lucid sentence structure and an exceptionally cognizant programming model. As a trademark at a new Python gathering verifies, the net outcome is that Python appears to "fit your cerebrum" that is, highlights of the language communicate in reliable and restricted manners and follow normally from a little arrangement of center ideas. This makes the language simpler to learn, comprehend, and recall. Practically speaking, Python software engineers don't have to continually allude to manuals when perusing or composing code; it's a reliably planned framework that many discover yields shockingly ordinary looking code.

By reasoning, Python embraces a fairly moderate methodology. This implies that in spite of the fact that there are typically various approaches to achieve a coding task, there is normally only one clear way, a couple of more subtle other options, and a little arrangement of reasonable collaborations wherever in the language. Also, Python doesn't settle on discretionary choices for you; when communications are vague, unequivocal mediation is liked over "wizardry." In the Python perspective, express is superior to implied, and basic is better compared to complex.

Past such plan subjects, Python incorporates devices, for example, modules and OOP that normally advance code reusability. Furthermore, in light of the fact that Python is centered on quality, so as well, normally, are Python software engineers.

1.1.3 Developer Productivity

During the incomparable Internet blast of the mid-to-late 1990s, it was hard to track down enough developers to carry out programming projects; engineers were approached to execute frameworks as quick as the Internet advanced. Today, in a time of cutbacks and monetary downturn, the image has moved. Programming staffs are regularly now requested to achieve similar errands with considerably less individuals.

In both of these situations, Python has sparkled as a device that permits developers to complete all the more less exertion. It is intentionally upgraded for speed of advancement its straightforward linguistic structure, dynamic composing, absence of gather steps, and underlying toolset permit software engineers to create programs in a small part of the time required when utilizing some different apparatuses. The net impact is that Python regularly helps designer efficiency ordinarily past the levels upheld by customary dialects. That is uplifting news in both win and fail times, and wherever the product business goes in the middle.

1.2 Is Python a "Scripting Language"?

Python is a broadly useful programming language that is regularly applied in scripting jobs. It is ordinarily characterized as an article arranged scripting language a definition that mixes support for OOP with a general direction toward scripting jobs. Truth be told, individuals frequently utilize "content" rather than "program" to depict a Python code record. In this book, the expressions "content" and "program" are utilized reciprocally, with a slight inclination for "content" to depict a less complex high level document and "program" to allude to a more modern multi file application.

Since the expression "scripting language" has such countless various implications to various spectators, some would incline toward that it not be applied to Python by any means. Indeed, individuals will in general make three totally different affiliations, some of which are more valuable than others, when they hear Python named in that capacity:

Shell tools: Some of the time when individuals hear Python depicted as a scripting language, they think it implies that Python is an instrument for coding working framework situated contents. Such programs are regularly dispatched from support order lines and perform undertakings such as preparing text records and dispatching different projects. Python projects can and do serve such jobs, however this is only one of many normal Python application spaces. It isn't only a superior shell-content language.

Control language: To other people, scripting alludes to a "stick" layer used to control and direct (i.e., content) other application segments. Python programs are without a doubt regularly conveyed in the setting of bigger applications. For example, to test equipment gadgets, Python projects may shout to segments that give low-level admittance to a gadget. Essentially, projects may run pieces of Python code at vital focuses to help end client item customization without the need to deliver and recompile the whole framework's source code.

Python's straightforwardness makes it a normally adaptable control device. In fact, however, this is likewise a typical Python job; many (maybe most) Python developers code independent contents while never utilizing or thinking about any coordinated segments. It isn't only a control language.

Ease of use: Likely the most ideal approach to think about the expression "scripting language" is that it alludes to a straightforward language utilized for rapidly coding errands. This is particularly evident when the term is applied to Python, which permits a lot quicker program advancement than aggregated dialects like C++. Its quick advancement cycle encourages an exploratory, steady method of programming that must be capable to be valued.

Try not to be tricked, however Python isn't only for basic assignments. Maybe, it makes assignments basic by its usability and adaptability. Python has a straightforward list of capabilities, however it permits projects to scale up in complexity depending on the situation. Thus, it is generally utilized for fast strategic undertakings and longer-term key turn of events.

Anyway, is Python a scripting language or not? It relies upon whom you inquire. When all is said in done, the expression "scripting" is likely best used to portray the fast and adaptable method of improvement that Python upholds, as opposed to a specific application area.

1.3 But what's the Downside?

Subsequent to utilizing it for a very long time and training it for 12, the solitary disadvantage to Python I've found is that, as presently carried out, its execution speed may not generally be pretty much as quick as that of gathered dialects like C and C++.

We'll discuss execution ideas in detail later in this book. To put it plainly, the standard executions of Python today order (i.e., make an interpretation of) source code articulations to a middle organization known as byte code and afterward decipher the byte code.

Byte code gives versatility, as it is a stage free arrangement. In any case, since Python isn't aggregated right down to parallel machine code (e.g., directions for an Intel chip), a few projects will run more gradually in Python than in a completely assembled language like C.

Regardless of whether you will at any point care about the execution speed contrast relies upon what sorts of projects you compose. Python has been streamlined various occasions, and Python code shows sufficiently quick to itself in most application spaces. Besides, at whatever point you accomplish something "genuine" in a Python content, such as preparing a record or building a graphical UI (GUI), your program will really run at C speed, since such assignments are promptly dispatched to gathered C code inside the Python mediator. All the more on a very basic level, Python's speed-of-advancement acquire is frequently undeniably more significant than any speed of execution misfortune, particularly given current PC speeds.

Indeed, even at the present CPU speeds, however, there still are a few spaces that do require ideal execution speeds. Numeric programming and movement, for instance, frequently need at any rate their center calculating segments to run at C speed (or better). On the off chance that you work in such a space, you can in any case utilize Python essentially split off the pieces of the application that require ideal speed into assembled expansions, and connection those into your framework for use in Python contents.

We will not discuss augmentations much in this content, however this is truly an example of the Python-as-control-language job we talked about before. A great representation of this double language system is the NumPy numeric programming expansion for Python; by consolidating assembled and enhanced numeric augmentation libraries with the Python language, NumPy transforms Python into a numeric programming apparatus that is proficient and simple to utilize.

You may never have to code such augmentations in your own Python work, yet they give an amazing enhancement component on the off chance that you at any point do.

1.4 Who Uses Python Today?

At this composition, the best gauge anybody can appear to make of the size of the Python client base is that there are approximately 1 million Python clients all throughout the planet today (give or take a couple). This gauge depends on different measurements, as download rates and designer reviews. Since Python is open source, a more careful check is troublesome there are no permit enrollments to count. Also, Python is consequently included with Linux disseminations, Macintosh PCs, and a few items and equipment, further blurring the client base picture.

All in all, however, Python appreciates a huge client base and an exceptionally dynamic engineer local area. Since Python has been around for about 19 years and has been generally utilized, it is likewise truly steady and vigorous. Other than being utilized by singular clients, Python is likewise being applied in genuine income creating items by genuine organizations.

For example:

- Google utilizes Python in its web search frameworks, and utilizes Python's maker.

- The YouTube video sharing assistance is to a great extent written in Python.

- The famous Bit Torrent distributed document sharing framework is a Python program.

- Google's famous App Engine web advancement structure utilizes Python as its application language.

- EVE Online, a Massively Multiplayer Online Game (MMOG), makes broad use of Python.

- Maya, an amazing incorporated 3D displaying and liveliness framework, gives a Python scripting API.

- Intel, Cisco, Hewlett-Packard, Seagate, Qualcomm, and IBM use Python for equipment testing.

- Industrial Light and Magic, Pixar, and others use Python in the creation of energized motion pictures.

- JPMorgan Chase, UBS, Getco, and Citadel apply Python for monetary market estimating.

- NASA, Los Alamos, Fermilab, JPL, and others use Python for logical programming undertakings.

- IRobot utilizes Python to create business automated gadgets.

- ESRI utilizes Python as an end-client customization device for its mainstream GIS planning items.

- The NSA utilizes Python for cryptography and knowledge examination.

- The Iron Port email worker item utilizes more than 1 million lines of Python code to manage its work.

- The One Laptop per Child (OLPC) project constructs its UI and movement model in Python.

Etc. Most likely the solitary consistent idea among the organizations utilizing Python today is that Python is utilized everywhere, regarding application spaces. Its broadly useful nature makes it material to practically all fields, not only one. Indeed, it's protected to say that essentially every generous association composing programming is utilizing Python, regardless of whether for transient strategic errands, like testing and organization, or for long haul vital item advancement. Python has demonstrated to function admirably in the two modes.

1.5 What Can I Do with Python?

As well as being a very much planned programming language, Python is valuable for achieving true undertakings such things designers do throughout each and every day.

It's regularly utilized in an assortment of areas, as an instrument for scripting different segments also, executing independent projects. Indeed, as a broadly useful language, Python's jobs are essentially limitless: you can utilize it for everything from site advancement and gaming to mechanical technology and shuttle control.

Be that as it may, the most well-known Python jobs at present appear to fall into a couple of general classifications. The following not many segments portray a portion of Python's most regular applications today, just as apparatuses utilized in every space. We will not have the option to investigate the instruments referenced here in any profundity in the event that you are keen on any of these points, see the Python site or different assets for additional subtleties.

1.5.1 Systems Programming

Python's implicit interfaces to working framework administrations make it ideal for composing convenient, viable framework organization devices and utilities (some of the time called shell apparatuses). Python projects can look through documents and index trees, dispatch different projects, do resemble handling with cycles and strings, etc.

Python's standard library accompanies POSIX ties and backing for all the typical OS instruments: climate factors, records, attachments, pipes, measures, numerous strings, normal articulation design coordinating, order line contentions, standard stream interfaces, shell order launchers, filename extension, and then some. What's more, the main part of Python's framework interfaces are intended to be versatile; for instance, a content that duplicates registry trees commonly runs unaltered on all significant Python stages. The Stack less Python framework, utilized by EVE Online, additionally offers progressed answers for multiprocessing necessities.

1.5.2 GUIs

Python's straightforwardness and quick turnaround additionally make it a decent counterpart for graphical UI programming. Python accompanies a standard article situated interface to the Tk GUI API called tkinter that permits Python projects to carry out compact GUIs with a local look and feel. Python/tkinter GUIs run unaltered on Microsoft Windows, X Windows (on UNIX and Linux), and the Mac OS (both Classic what's more, OS X). A free augmentation bundle, PMW, adds progressed gadgets to the tkinter tool compartment. Furthermore, the wxPython GUI API, in view of a C++ library, offers an option tool compartment for building convenient GUIs in Python.

More elevated level tool compartments, for example, PythonCard and Dabo are based on top of base APIs like wxPython and tkinter. With the appropriate library, you can likewise utilize GUI support in other tool compartments in Python, for example, Qt with PyQt, GTK with PyGTK, MFC with PyWin32, .NET with IronPython, and Swing with Jython (the Java adaptation of Python) or JPype. For applications that run in internet browsers or have straightforward interface necessities, both Jython and Python web structures and worker side CGI contents, portrayed in the following segment, give extra UI alternatives.

1.5.3 Internet Scripting

Python accompanies standard Internet modules that permit Python projects to play out a wide assortment of systems administration errands, in customer and worker modes. Contents can impart over attachments; extricate structure data shipped off worker side CGI contents; move documents by FTP; parse, create, and investigate XML records; send, get, form, and parse email; bring website pages by URLs; parse the HTML and XML of got site pages; convey over XML-RPC, SOAP, and Telnet; and that's only the tip of the iceberg. Python's libraries make these assignments strikingly basic.

Also, an enormous assortment of outsider instruments are accessible on the Web for doing Web programming in Python. For example, the HTMLGen framework creates HTML records from Python class based depictions, the mod python bundle runs Python proficiently inside the Apache web worker and supports worker side template with its Python Server Pages, and the Jython framework accommodates consistent Python/Java coordination and supports coding of worker side applets that sudden spike in demand for customers.

Moreover, out and out web advancement system bundles for Python, for example, Django, TurboGears, web2py, Pylons, Zope, and WebWare, support fast development of full-included and creation quality sites with Python. A large number of these incorporate highlights, for example, object-social mappers, a Model/View/Controller design, worker side scripting and template, and AJAX support, to give total and endeavor level web advancement arrangements.

1.5.4 Component Integration

We talked about the segment coordination job prior while portraying Python as a control language. Python's capacity to be reached out by and installed in C and C++ frameworks makes it valuable as an adaptable paste language for scripting the conduct of different frameworks and parts. For example, coordinating a C library into Python empowers Python to test and dispatch the library's segments, and inserting Python in an item empowers on location customizations to be coded without having to recompile the whole item (or transport its source code by any means).

Devices, for example, the SWIG and SIP code generators can robotize a significant part of the work expected to connect incorporated parts into Python for use in contents, and the Cython framework permits coders to blend Python and C-like code. Bigger systems, for example, Python's COM support on Windows, the Jython Java-based execution, the Iron Python .NET based execution, and different CORBA tool box for Python, give elective approaches to content segments. On Windows, for instance, Python contents can utilize systems to content Word and Excel.

1.5.5 Database Programming

For conventional information base requests, there are Python interfaces to all ordinarily utilized social data set frameworks Sybase, Oracle, Informix, ODBC, MySQL, PostgreSQL, SQLite, and that's just the beginning. The Python world has additionally characterized a compact data set API for getting to SQL information base frameworks from Python contents, which appears to be identical on an assortment of basic data set frameworks. For example, on the grounds that the seller interfaces carry out the versatile API, a content written to work with the free MySQL framework will work to a great extent unaltered on different frameworks (like Oracle); you should simply supplant the under lying merchant interface.

Python's standard pickle module gives a basic item steadiness framework it permits projects to effortlessly save and reestablish whole Python objects to records and document like articles.

On the Web, you'll likewise track down an outsider open source framework named ZODB that gives a total article arranged data set framework for Python contents, and others (like SQLObject and SQLAlchemy) that map social tables onto Python's class model. Besides, as of Python, the in-measure SQLite implanted SQL information base motor is a standard piece of Python itself.

1.5.6 Rapid Prototyping

To Python programs, parts written in Python and C appear to be identical. In light of this current, it's feasible to model frameworks in Python at first, and afterward move chosen segments to an incorporated language like C or C++ for conveyance. Not at all like some prototyping apparatuses, doesn't Python need a total revise once the model has set. Portions of the framework that don't need the effectiveness of a language, for example, C++ can remain coded in Python for simplicity of support and use.

1.5.7 Numeric and Scientific Programming

The NumPy numeric programming augmentation for Python referenced before incorporates such progressed devices as an exhibit object, interfaces to standard numerical libraries, furthermore, substantially more. By coordinating Python with numeric schedules coded in an accumulated language for speed, NumPy transforms Python into a refined at this point simple to utilize numeric programming device that can regularly supplant existing code written in customary incorporated dialects like FORTRAN or C++. Extra numeric instruments for Python support liveliness, 3D representation, equal handling, etc. The famous SciPy and Scientific Python augmentations, for instance, give extra libraries of logical programming devices and use NumPy code.

1.5.8 Gaming, Images, Serial Ports, XML, Robots, and More

Python is usually applied in a greater number of spaces than can be referenced here. For instance, you can do:

- Game programming and sight and sound in Python with the pygame framework.

- Serial port correspondence on Windows, Linux, and more with the PySerial expansion.

- Image handling with PIL, PyOpenGL, Blender, Maya, and others.

- Robot control programming with the PyRo tool stash.

- XML parsing with the xml library bundle, the xmlrpclib module, and outsider expansions.

- Artificial insight programming with neural organization test systems and master framework shells.

- Natural language investigation with the NLTK bundle.

You can even play solitaire with the PySol program. You'll discover support for some such fields at the PyPI sites, and through web look.

A significant number of these particular spaces are to a great extent occasions of Python's segment incorporation job in real life once more. Adding it as a frontend to libraries of segments written in an incorporated language, for example, C makes Python helpful for scripting in a wide assortment of spaces. As a broadly useful language that upholds reconciliation, Python is generally pertinent.

1.6 How Is Python Supported?

As a well-known open source framework, Python appreciates a huge and dynamic improvement local area that reacts to issues and creates upgrades with a speed that numerous business programming designers would discover surprising (if not absolutely stunning).

Python engineers facilitate work online with a source-control framework. Changes follow a proper PEP (Python Enhancement Proposal) convention and should be joined by expansions to Python's broad relapse testing framework. Indeed, adjusting Python today is generally pretty much as included as changing business programming a long ways from Python's initial days, when an email to its maker would get the job done, however something worth being thankful for given its present huge client base.

The PSF (Python Software Foundation), a conventional charitable gathering, coordinates meetings and manages protected innovation issues. Various Python meetings are held all throughout the planet; O'Reilly's OSCON and the PSF's PyCon are the biggest. The previous of these tends to numerous open source projects, and the last is a Python-just occasion that has encountered solid development lately. Participation at PyCon 2008 almost multiplied from the earlier year, developing from 586 participants in 2007 to more than 1,000 of every 2008. This was closely following a 40% participation expansion in 2007, from 410 out of 2006. PyCon 2009 had 943 participants, a slight lessening from 2008, yet a still solid appearing during a worldwide downturn.

1.7 What Are Python's Technical Strengths?

Normally, this is a designer's inquiry. On the off chance that you don't as of now have a programming foundation, the language in the following not many areas might be somewhat bewildering don't stress, we'll investigate these terms in more detail as we continue through this book. For engineers, however, here is a fast prologue to a portion of Python's top specialized highlights.

1.7.1 It's Object-Oriented

Python is an article situated language, from the beginning. Its class model backings progressed ideas like polymorphism, administrator over-burdening, and numerous legacy; yet, with regards to Python's straightforward language structure and composing, OOP is surprisingly simple to apply. Indeed, in the event that you don't comprehend these terms, you'll see they are a lot simpler to learn with Python than with pretty much some other OOP language accessible.

Other than filling in as an amazing code organizing and reuse gadget, Python's OOP nature makes it ideal as a scripting instrument for object-arranged frameworks dialects like C++ and Java. For instance, with the fitting paste code, Python projects can subclass (practice) classes carried out in C++, Java, and C#.

Of equivalent importance, OOP is a choice in Python; you can go far without having to become an article master at the same time. Similar as C++, Python upholds both procedural furthermore, object-situated programming modes. Its article situated apparatuses can be applied if also, when imperatives permit. This is particularly valuable in strategic improvement modes, which block configuration stages.

1.7.2 It's Free

Python is totally allowed to utilize and disperse. Likewise with other open source programming, like Tcl, Perl, Linux, and Apache, you can bring the whole Python framework's source code for nothing on the Internet. There are no limitations on duplicating it, implanting it in your frameworks, or delivery it with your items. Truth be told, you can even sell Python's source code, in the event that you are so disposed.

However, don't misunderstand the thought: "free" doesn't signify "unsupported." actually, the Python online local area reacts to client inquiries with a speed that most business programming assist work areas with doing attempt to imitate. Also, on the grounds that Python accompanies total source code, it engages designers, prompting the formation of an enormous group of execution specialists. Despite the fact that considering or changing a writing computer programs language's execution isn't actually a good time for everyone, it's encouraging to realize that you can do as such on the off chance that you need to. You're not reliant on the impulses of a business seller; a definitive documentation source is available to you.

As referenced before, Python advancement is performed by a local area that generally facilitates its endeavors over the Internet. It comprises of Python's maker Guido van Rossum, the authoritatively blessed Benevolent Dictator forever (BDFL) of Python in addition to a supporting cast of thousands. Language changes should follow a conventional upgrade strategy and be examined by both different designers and the BDFL. Cheerfully, this will in general make Python more moderate with changes than some different dialects.

1.7.3 It is Portable

The standard execution of Python is written in convenient ANSI C, and it gathers and runs on basically every significant stage as of now being used. For instance, Python programs run today on everything from PDAs to supercomputers. As a fractional rundown, Python is accessible on:

• Linux and UNIX frameworks

• Microsoft Windows and DOS (every single current flavor)

• Mac OS (both OS X and Classic)

• BeOS, OS/2, VMS, and QNX

• Real-time frameworks like VxWorks

• Cray supercomputers and IBM centralized computers

• PDAs running Palm OS, PocketPC, and Linux

• Cell telephones running Symbian OS and Windows Mobile

• Gaming consoles and iPods

• And more

Like the language mediator itself, the standard library modules that transport with Python are carried out to be as convenient across stage limits as could really be expected. Further, Python programs are consequently ordered to versatile byte code, which runs something similar on any stage with a viable variant of Python introduced (more on this in the following section).

This means Python programs utilizing the center language and standard libraries run something very similar on Linux, Windows, and most different frameworks with a Python mediator. Most Python ports likewise contain stage explicit expansions (e.g., COM support on Windows), however the center Python language and libraries work the equivalent all over the place. As referenced before, Python additionally incorporates an interface to the Tk GUI tool stash called tkinter, which permits Python projects to carry out full-highlighted graphical UIs that sudden spike in demand for all.

1.7.4 It is Powerful

From a highlights point of view, Python is something of a half and half. Its toolset places it between conventional scripting dialects (like Tcl, Scheme, and Perl) and frameworks improvement dialects (like C, C++, and Java). Python gives all the straightforwardness furthermore, convenience of a scripting language, alongside further developed computer programming instruments regularly found in aggregated dialects. In contrast to some scripting dialects, this blend makes Python valuable for enormous scope advancement projects. As a see, here are a portion of the principle things you'll discover in Python's tool compartment:

Dynamic typing: Python monitors the sorts of items your program utilizes when it runs; it doesn't need muddled sort and size announcements in your code. Truth be told, as you'll find in later chapter, there is nothing of the sort as a kind or variable announcement anyplace in Python. Since Python code doesn't compel information types, it is moreover typically consequently pertinent to an entire scope of items.

Automatic memory management: Python naturally dispenses protests and recovers ("trash gathers") them at the point when they are not, at this point utilized, and most can develop and shrivel on request. As you'll learn, Python monitors low-level memory subtleties so you don't need to.

Programming in the large support: For building bigger frameworks, Python incorporates apparatuses like modules, classes, and exemptions. These instruments permit you to coordinate frameworks into segments, use OOP to reuse and alter code, and handle occasions and blunders effortlessly.

Built in object types: Python gives regularly utilized information designs like records, word references, and strings as inherent pieces of the language; as you'll see, they're both adaptable and simple to utilize. For example, implicit articles can develop and recoil on request, can be subjectively settled to address complex data, and that's just the beginning.

Built-in tools: To handle every one of those article types, Python accompanies incredible and standard tasks, including link (joining assortments), cutting (separating areas), arranging, planning, and that's only the tip of the iceberg.

Library utilities: For more explicit errands, Python likewise accompanies an enormous assortment of pre coded library devices that help everything from standard articulation coordinating to systems administration. When you become familiar with the actual language, Python's library apparatuses are the place where a significant part of the application-level activity happens.

Third-party utilities: Since Python is open source, engineers are urged to contribute pre coded instruments that help assignments past those upheld by its assembled (ins); on the Web, you'll discover free help for COM, imaging, CORBA ORBs, XML, information base access, and significantly more.

Notwithstanding the variety of apparatuses in Python, it holds a strikingly straightforward grammar and plan. The outcome is an incredible programming apparatus with all the convenience of a scripting language.

1.7.5 It is Mixable

Python projects can undoubtedly be "stuck" to parts written in different dialects in an assortment of ways. For instance, Python's C API lets C projects call and be called by Python programs deftly. That implies you can add usefulness to the Python framework depending on the situation, and use Python programs inside different conditions or frameworks.

Blending Python in with libraries coded in dialects like C or C++, for example, makes it a simple to-utilize frontend language and customization device. As referenced before, this additionally makes Python great at fast prototyping; frameworks might be carried out in Python first, to use its speed of advancement, and later moved to C for conveyance, each piece in turn, as indicated by execution requests.

1.7.6 It is Easy to Use

To run a Python program, you just sort it and run it. There are no transitional arrange and interface steps, as there are for dialects like C or C++. Python executes programs quickly, which makes for an intelligent programming experience and fast turnaround after program changes as a rule, you can observer the impact of a program change as quick as possible sort it.

Obviously, advancement cycle turnaround is just a single part of Python's convenience. It additionally gives a purposely straightforward sentence structure and incredible inherent apparatuses. Truth be told, a few have ventured to such an extreme as to call Python "executable pseudo code." Because it dispenses with a significant part of the intricacy in different apparatuses, Python programs are easier, more modest, and more adaptable than identical projects in dialects like C, C++, and Java.

1.7.7 It is Easy to learn

This carries us to a central issue of this book: contrasted with other programming dialects, the center Python language is strikingly simple to learn. Truth be told, you can hope to code huge Python programs surprisingly fast (or maybe in not more than hours, in case you're as of now an accomplished developer). That is uplifting news for proficient designers looking to get familiar with the language to use at work, just as for end clients of frameworks that uncover a Python layer for customization or control.

Today, numerous frameworks depend on the way that end clients can rapidly learn sufficient Python to tailor their Python customizations' code nearby, with practically zero help. In spite of the fact that Python has progressed programming instruments, its center language will in any case appear to be easy to amateurs and masters the same.

1.7.8 It is named after Monty Python

Alright, this isn't exactly a specialized strength, however it is by all accounts a shockingly very much maintained mystery that I wish to uncover in advance. Notwithstanding all the reptile symbols in the Python world, in all actuality Python maker Guido van Rossum named it after the BBC satire arrangement Monty Python's Flying Circus. He is a major fanatic of Monty Python, as are numerous product engineers (for sure, there appears to nearly be an evenness between the two fields).

This inheritance definitely adds a hilarious quality to Python code models. For example, the conventional "foo" and "bar" for nonexclusive variable names become "spam" and "eggs" in the Python world. An intermittent "Brian," "ni," and "growth" in like manner owe their appearances to this namesake. It even effects the Python people group everywhere: talks at Python meetings are routinely charged as "The Spanish Inquisition."

The entirety of this is, obviously, exceptionally clever on the off chance that you know about the show, however less so something else. You don't should be comfortable with the arrangement to figure out models that get references to Monty Python (counting numerous you will find in this book), yet in any event you presently know their root.

1.8 How Does Python Stack Up to Language X?

At long last, to put it with regards to what you may definitely know, individuals here and there contrast Python with dialects like Perl, Tcl, and Java. We discussed execution before, so here we'll zero in on usefulness. While different dialects are likewise valuable instruments to know and utilize, numerous individuals find that Python:

• Is more remarkable than Tcl. Python's help for "programming in the enormous" makes it relevant to the improvement of bigger frameworks.

• Has a cleaner punctuation and less difficult plan than Perl, which makes it more lucid also, viable and decreases program bugs.

• Is more straightforward and simpler to use than Java. Python is a scripting language, however Java acquires a significant part of the intricacy and punctuation of frameworks dialects like C++.

• Is less complex and simpler to use than C++, yet it doesn't frequently rival C++; as a scripting language, Python normally serves various jobs.

• Is both more remarkable and more cross-stage than Visual Basic. Its open source nature likewise implies it isn't constrained by a solitary organization.

- Is more clear and universally useful than PHP. Python is here and there used to build sites, but on the other hand it's broadly utilized in essentially every other PC area, from mechanical technology to film activity.

- Is more developed and has a more coherent linguistic structure than Ruby. In contrast to Ruby and Java, OOP is a choice in Python, Python doesn't force OOP on clients or undertakings to which it may not have any significant bearing.

- Has the unique kind of dialects like Small Talk and Lisp, yet in addition has a basic, customary language structure available to designers just as end clients of adjustable frameworks.

Particularly for programs that accomplish more than check text records, and that may must be use later on by others (or by you!), numerous individuals find that Python possesses all the necessary qualities better than some other scripting or programming language accessible today. Moreover, except if your application requires top execution, Python is regularly a feasible option in contrast to frameworks improvement dialects, for example, C, C++, and Java: Python code will be substantially less hard to compose, troubleshoot, and keep up.

Obviously, your creator has been a card-conveying Python evangelist since 1992, so accept these remarks as you may. They do, notwithstanding, mirror the normal experience of numerous engineers who have set aside effort to investigate what Python has to bring to the table.

1.9 Chapter Summary

1. Programming quality, engineer efficiency, program movability, support libraries, part coordination, and straightforward satisfaction. Of these, the quality and profitability topics appear to be the fundamental reasons that individuals decide to utilize Python.

2. Google, Industrial Light and Magic, EVE Online, Jet Propulsion Labs, Maya, ESRI, also, some more. Pretty much every association doing programming improvement utilizes Python in some design, regardless of whether for long haul key item advancement or for transient strategic undertakings like testing and framework organization.

3. Python's drawback is execution: it will not run as fast as completely arranged dialects like C and C++. Then again, it's fast enough for most applications, and commonplace Python code runs at near C speed in any case since it summon connected in C code in the translator. On the off chance that speed is basic, incorporated augmentations are accessible for calculating pieces of an application.

4. You can utilize Python for almost anything you can do with a PC, from site improvement and gaming to advanced mechanics and shuttle control.

5. Import this triggers an Easter egg inside Python that shows a portion of the plan methods of reasoning basic the language. You'll figure out how to run this proclamation in the following part

6. "Spam" is a reference from a well-known Monty Python production in which individuals attempting to request food in a cafeteria are muffled by an ensemble of Vikings singing about spam. Goodness, and it's likewise a typical variable name in Python contents.

1.10 Python Is Engineering, Not Art

At the point when Python previously arose on the product scene in the mid-1990s, it brought forth the thing is presently something of an exemplary struggle between its defenders and those of another well-known scripting language, Perl. By and by, I think the discussion is drained and inappropriate today designers are sufficiently brilliant to make their own inferences. All things considered, this is perhaps the most well-known themes I'm gotten some information about on the preparation street, so it appears to be fitting to say a couple of words regarding it here.

The short story is this: you can do everything in Python that you can in Perl, yet you can peruse your code after you do it. That is it their areas generally cover, yet Python is more centered on creating discernible code. For some, the improved intelligibility of Python means better code reusability and practicality, settling on Python a superior decision for programs that won't be composed once and discarded. Perl code is not difficult to compose, however hard to peruse. Given that most programming has a life expectancy any longer than its underlying creation, many consider Python to be a more compelling device.

To some degree longer story mirrors the foundations of the fashioners of the two dialects and underscores a portion of the fundamental reasons individuals decide to utilize Python. Python's maker is a mathematician via preparing; in that capacity, he created a language with a serious level of consistency its sentence structure and toolset are surprisingly rational. Also, similar to math, Python's plan is symmetrical the greater part of the language follows from a little arrangement of center ideas. For example, when one handles Python's kind of polymorphism, the rest is generally subtleties.

On the other hand, the maker of the Perl language is an etymologist, and its plan mirrors this legacy. There are numerous approaches to achieve similar errands in Perl, and language develops communicate in setting touchy and now and again very unobtrusive ways similar as common language. As the notable Perl witticism expresses, "There's more than one approach to do it." Given this plan, both the Perl language and its client local area have generally energized opportunity of articulation when composing code. One individual's Perl code can be profoundly not the same as another's. Indeed, composing special, interesting code is regularly a wellspring of pride among Perl clients.

In any case, as any individual who has done any significant code support ought to have the option to bear witness to, opportunity of articulation is incredible for craftsmanship, yet inferior for designing. In designing, we need an insignificant list of capabilities and consistency. In designing, opportunity of articulation can prompt upkeep bad dreams. As more than one Perl client has trusted to me, the consequence of an excess of opportunity is regularly code that is a lot simpler to revamp without any preparation than to change.

Think about this: when individuals make a composition or a model, they do as such for themselves for absolutely stylish purposes. The chance of another person changing that painting or figure later doesn't go into it. This is a basic contrast among workmanship and designing. At the point when individuals compose programming, they are not composing it for themselves.

Truth be told, they are not in any event, composing basically for the PC. Maybe, great developers realize that code is composed for the following individual who needs to peruse it to keep up or reuse it. In the event that that individual can't comprehend the code, it's everything except pointless in a sensible improvement situation.

This is the place where numerous individuals find that Python most unmistakably separates itself from scripting dialects like Perl. Since Python's linguistic structure model nearly powers clients to compose comprehensible code, Python programs loan themselves all the more straightforwardly to the full programming improvement cycle. What's more, since Python underlines thoughts like restricted collaborations, code consistency and routineness, and highlight consistency, it all the more straightforwardly encourages code that can be utilized long after it is first composed.

Over the long haul, Python's attention on code quality in itself supports developer efficiency, just as software engineer fulfillment. Python software engineers can be innovative, as well, obviously, and as we'll see, the language offers various answers for certain assignments. At its center, however, Python supports great designing in manners that other scripting dialects frequently don't.

At any rate, that is the basic agreement among numerous individuals who have received Python. You ought to consistently pass judgment on such cases for yourself, obviously, by realizing what Python has to bring to the table. To assist you with beginning, how about we proceed onward to the following part.

Chapter 2. How Python Runs Programs

This part and the following investigate program execution how you dispatch code, and how Python runs. In this part, we'll study the Python translator.

This part will at that point tell you the best way to get your own projects fully operational. Startup subtleties are innately stage explicit, and a portion of the material in these two sections may not matter to the stage you work on, so you should don't hesitate to skip parts not pertinent to your proposed use. Moreover, further developed users who have utilized comparable instruments before and like to get to the meat of the language rapidly might need to document a portion of this section as "for future reference." For most of you, how about we figure out how to run some code.

2.1 Introducing the Python Interpreter

Up until now, I've for the most part been discussing Python as a programming language. However, as right now executed, it's likewise a product bundle called a translator. A translator is a sort of program that executes different projects. At the point when you compose a Python program, the Python mediator peruses your program and does the directions it contains.

In actuality, the translator is a layer of programming rationale between your code and the PC equipment on your machine.

At the point when the Python bundle is introduced on your machine, it creates various segments insignificantly, a translator and a help library. Contingent upon how you use it, the Python translator may appear as an executable program, or a bunch of libraries connected into another program. Contingent upon which kind of Python you run, the actual mediator might be executed as a C program, a bunch of Java classes, or something different. Whatever structure it takes, the Python code you compose should consistently be controlled by this mediator. Furthermore, to empower that, you should introduce a Python mediator on your PC.

Python establishment subtleties shift by stage and are canvassed in more profundity in Appendix A. In short:

• Windows clients get and run a self-introducing executable document that puts Python on their machines. Basically double tap and say Yes or next at all prompts.

• Linux and Mac OS X clients likely as of now have a usable Python preinstalled on their PCs it's a standard part on these stages today.

• Some Linux and Mac OS X clients (and most UNIX clients) incorporate Python from its full source code appropriation bundle.

• Linux clients can likewise discover RPM documents, and Mac OS X clients can discover different Mac explicit establishment bundles.

• Other stages have establishment procedures applicable to those stages. For example, Python is accessible on cells, game consoles, and iPods, yet establishment subtleties differ generally.

Python itself might be gotten from the download page on the site. It might likewise be found through different other dissemination channels. Remember that you ought to consistently verify whether Python is as of now present prior to introducing it. In case you're dealing with Windows, you'll as a rule discover Python in the Start menu, as caught in Figure 1 (these menu choices are talked about in the following part).

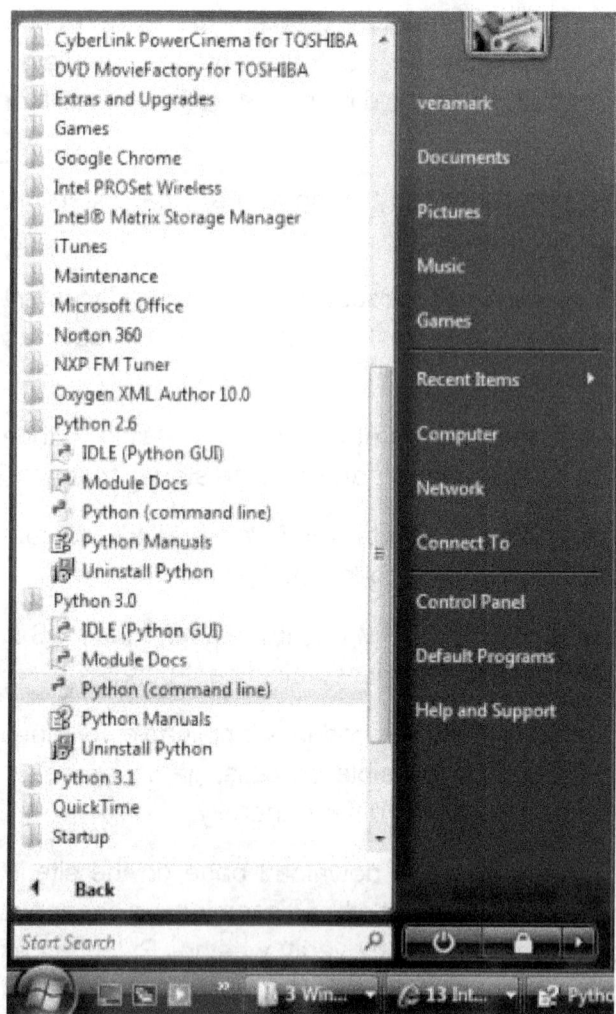

(Figure 1: At the point when introduced on Windows, this is the way Python appears in your Start button menu)

On UNIX and Linux, Python likely lives in your/usr index tree. Since establishment subtleties are so stage explicit, we'll artfulness the remainder of this story here. For additional subtleties on the establishment interaction, counsel Appendix A. For the motivations behind this section and the following, I'll accept that you have Python all set.

2.2 Program Execution

Writing and run a Python content relies upon whether you view at these undertakings as a software engineer, or as a Python translator. The two perspectives offer significant viewpoints on Python programming.

2.2.1 The Programmer's View

In its easiest structure, a Python program is only a content document containing Python proclamations.

For instance, the accompanying document, named script0.py, is one of the least difficult Python contents. I could conjure up, however it passes for a completely utilitarian Python program.

This document contains two Python print articulations, which just print a string (the content in cites) and a numeric articulation result (2 to the force 100) to the yield stream.

Try not to stress over the linguistic structure of this code yet for this section, we're intrigued as it were in getting it to run. I'll clarify the print explanation, and why you can raise 2 to the power 100 in Python without flooding, in the following pieces of this book.

You can make such a document of articulations with any content manager you like. By show,

Python program documents are given names that end in .py; in fact, this naming plan is required uniquely for records that are "imported," as shown later in this book, yet most Python records have .py names for consistency.

After you've composed these articulations into a book document, you should advise Python to execute the record which essentially intends to run every one of the assertions in the record through and through, in a steady progression. As you'll find in the following part, you can dispatch Python program documents by shell order lines, by clicking their symbols, from inside IDEs, and with other standard methods. In the event that all works out positively, when you execute the record, you'll see the consequences of the two print articulations appear some place on your PC naturally, ordinarily in a similar window you were in when you ran the program.

For instance, this is what happened when I ran this content from a DOS order line on a Windows PC (commonly called a Command Prompt window, found in the Accessories program menu), to ensure it didn't have any senseless grammatical errors.

We've quite recently run a Python content that prints a string and a number. We presumably will not win any programming grants with this code, yet it's sufficient to catch the essentials of program execution.

2.2.2 Python's View

The short depiction in the earlier segment is genuinely standard for scripting dialects, and it's typically all that most Python software engineers require to know. You type code into text documents, and you run those records through the translator. In the engine, however, somewhat more happens when you advise Python to "go." Although information on Python internals isn't rigorously needed for Python programming, a fundamental comprehension of the runtime design of Python can help you handle the master plan of program execution.

At the point when you educate Python to run your content, there are a couple of steps that Python completes before your code really begins crunching ceaselessly. In particular, it's originally arranged to something many refer to as "byte code" and afterward steered to something many refer to as a "virtual machine."

Byte code compilation: Inside, and totally stowed away from you, when you execute a program Python initially orders your source code (the assertions in your record) into a configuration known as byte code. Assemblage is basically an interpretation step, and byte code is a lower-level, stage free portrayal of your source code. Generally, Python interprets every one of your source proclamations into a gathering of byte code guidelines by disintegrating them into singular advances. This byte code interpretation is performed to speed execution byte code can be run considerably more rapidly than the first source code explanations in your content document.

You'll see that the earlier passage said that this is totally stowed away from you. In the event that the Python interaction has compose access on your machine, it will store the byte code of your projects in records that end with a .pyc expansion (".pyc" signifies ordered ".py" source). You will see these documents appear on your PC after you've run a couple of projects close by the relating source code records (that is, in the equivalent catalogs).

Python saves byte code like this as a startup speed enhancement. The following time you run your program, Python will stack the .pyc documents and skirt the arrangement venture, as long as you haven't changed your source code since the byte code was last saved. Python naturally checks the timestamps of source and byte code records to know when it must recompile on the off chance that you resave your source code, byte code is consequently reproduced the following time your program is run.

On the off chance that Python can't compose the byte code documents to your machine, your program actually works the byte code is created in memory and basically disposed of on program exit.

Be that as it may, on the grounds that .pyc records speed startup time, you'll need to ensure they are composed for bigger projects. Byte code records are additionally one approach to send Python programs Python is glad to run a program if everything it can discover are .pyc documents, regardless of whether the first .py source records are missing.

The Python Virtual Machine (PVM): When your program has been gathered to byte code (or the byte code has been stacked from existing .pyc documents), it is sent off for execution to something by and large known as the Python Virtual Machine (PVM, for the more abbreviation slanted among you). The PVM sounds more amazing than it is; truly, it is anything but a different program, and it need not be introduced without help from anyone else. Indeed, the PVM is only a major circle that emphasizes through your byte code guidelines, individually, to complete their tasks. The PVM is the run time motor of Python; it's consistently present as a feature of the Python framework, and the segment genuinely runs your contents. In fact, it's simply the last advance of what is known as the "Python mediator."

Figure 2 delineates the runtime structure portrayed here. Remember that the entirety of this intricacy is purposely stowed away from Python software engineers. Byte code accumulation is programmed, and the PVM is simply important for the Python framework that you have introduced on your machine. Once more, developers just code and run records of explanations.

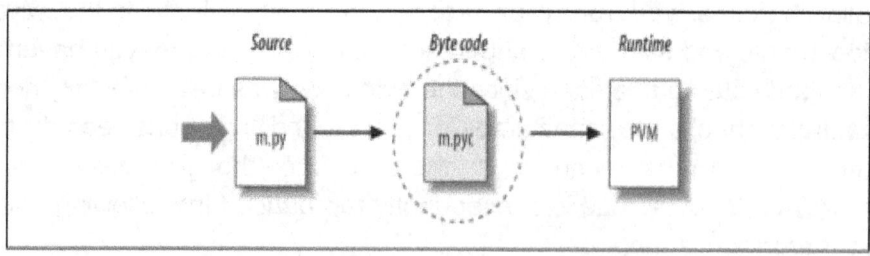

Figure 2. Python's traditional runtime execution model

Performance implications: Readers with a foundation in completely assembled dialects, for example, C and C++ may see a couple of contrasts in the Python model. For a certain something, there is normally no form or "make" step in Python work: code pursues quickly it is composed. For another, Python byte code isn't parallel machine code (e.g., directions for an Intel chip). Byte code is a Python explicit portrayal.

This is the reason some Python code may not run as quick as C or C++ code, as portrayed in past section the PVM circle, not the CPU chip, actually should decipher the byte code, and byte code guidelines require more work than CPU directions. Then again, dissimilar to in exemplary translators, there is as yet an inside assemble step Python doesn't have to reanalyze and reparse each source explanation more than once. The net impact is that unadulterated Python code runs at speeds somewhere close to those of a conventional incorporated language and a customary deciphered language. See past section for additional on Python execution tradeoffs.

Development implications: Another consequence of Python's execution model is that there is actually no qualification between the turn of events and execution conditions. That is, the frameworks that order and execute your source code are truly very much the same. This likeness may have somewhat more importance to users with a foundation in customary arranged dialects, however in Python, the compiler is consistently present at runtime and is essential for the framework that runs programs.

This makes for a considerably more quick advancement cycle. There is no compelling reason to precompile and interface before execution may start; basically type and run the code. This additionally adds a significantly more unique flavor to the language it is conceivable, and frequently exceptionally advantageous, for Python projects to develop and execute other Python programs at runtime. The eval and executive fabricated ins, for example, acknowledge and run strings containing Python program code. This design is additionally why Python fits item customization since Python code can be changed on the fly, clients can adjust the Python parts of a framework on location without expecting to have or order the whole framework's code.

At a more crucial level, remember that all we truly have in Python is runtime there is no underlying gather time stage by any means, and everything occurs as the program is running. This even incorporates tasks like the making of capacities and classes and the linkage of modules. Such occasions happen before execution in more static dialects, yet occur as projects execute in Python. As we'll see, the net impact makes for a substantially more powerful programming experience than that to which a few per users might be acclimated.

2.3 Execution Model Variations

Prior to proceeding onward, I should bring up that the inner execution stream depicted in the earlier area mirrors the standard execution of Python today yet isn't actually a prerequisite of the Python language itself. Thus, the execution model is inclined to changing with time. Truth be told, there are as of now a couple of frameworks that adjust the image in Figure 2 to some degree. How about we take a couple of seconds to investigate the most unmistakable of these varieties.

2.3.1 Python Implementation Alternatives

Truly, as this book is being composed, there are three essential executions of the Python language CPython, Jython, and Iron Python alongside a small bunch of optional executions like Stack less Python. In short, CPython is the standard execution; all the others have quite certain reasons and jobs. All carry out a similar Python language yet execute programs in an unexpected way.

CPython: The first, and standard, execution of Python is normally called CPython, when you need to balance it with the other two. Its name comes from the way that it is coded in convenient ANSI C language code. This is the Python that you get from site, get with the Active Python dispersion, and have consequently on most Linux and Mac OS X machines. In the event that you've discovered a preinstalled rendition of Python on your machine, it's presumably CPython, except if your organization is utilizing Python in very specific ways.

Except if you need to content Java or .NET applications with Python, you presumably need to utilize the standard CPython framework. Since it is the reference execution of the language, it will in general run the quickest, be the most complete, and be more powerful than the elective frameworks. Figure 2 mirrors CPython's runtime design.

Jython: The Jython framework (initially known as JPython) is an elective execution of the Python language, directed for joining with the Java programming language.

jython comprises of Java classes that arrange Python source code to Java byte code and afterward course the subsequent byte code to the Java Virtual Machine (JVM). Developers actually code Python articulations in .py text documents obviously; the Jython situation basically replaces the furthest right two air pockets in Figure 2 with Java based counterparts.

Jython will likely permit Python code to content Java applications, much as CPython permits Python to content C and C++ parts. Its coordination with Java is strikingly consistent. Since Python code is meant Java byte code, it closely resembles a genuine Java program at runtime. Jython contents can fill in as web applets and servlets, assemble Java based GUIs, etc. In addition, Jython incorporates coordination support that permits Python code to import and utilize Java classes like they were coded in Python. Since Jython is increasingly slow hearty than CPython, however, it is normally seen as an apparatus of interest principally to Java designers searching for a scripting language to be a frontend to Java code.

Iron Python: A third execution of Python, and more up to date than both CPython and Jython, Iron Python is intended to permit Python projects to incorporate with applications coded to work with Microsoft's .NET Framework for Windows, just as the Mono open source identical for Linux. .NET and its C# programming language runtime framework are intended to be a language-unbiased item correspondence layer, in the soul of Microsoft's prior COM model. Iron Python permits Python projects to go about as both customer and worker parts, open from other .NET dialects.

By execution, Iron Python is actually similar to Jython (and, truth be told, was created by a similar maker) it replaces the last two air pockets in Figure 2-2 with counterparts for execution in the .NET climate. Likewise, as Jython, Iron Python has an exceptional center it is essentially important to designers incorporating Python with .NET segments. Since it is being created by Microsoft, however, Iron Python may likewise have the option to use some significant improvement instruments for better execution. Iron Python's degree is as yet developing as I compose this; for additional subtleties, counsel the Python online assets or search the Web.

2.3.2 Execution Optimization Tools

CPython, Jython, and Iron Python all execute the Python language correspondingly: by aggregating source code to byte code and executing the byte code on a suitable virtual machine. Then again different frameworks, incorporating the Psyco in the nick of time compiler and the Shedskin C++ interpreter, rather endeavor to streamline the fundamental execution model. These frameworks are not needed information now in your Python profession, however a brief glance at their spot in the execution model may help demystify the model by and large.

The Psyco just in time compiler: The Psyco framework isn't another Python execution, yet rather a part that expands the byte code execution model to make programs run quicker. As far as Figure 2, Psyco is an improvement to the PVM that gathers and uses type data while the program hurries to interpret segments of the program's byte code right down to genuine parallel machine code for quicker execution. Psyco achieves this interpretation without expecting changes to the code or a different arrangement venture during improvement.

Generally, while your program runs, Psyco gathers data about the sorts of items being passed around; that data can be utilized to create profoundly productive machine code custom fitted for those article types. When produced, the machine code at that point replaces the comparing a piece of the first byte code to speed your program's general execution. The net impact is that, with Psyco, your program turns out to be a lot faster after some time and as it is running. In ideal cases, some Python code may become as quick as aggregated C code under Psyco.

Since this interpretation from byte code occurs at program runtime, Psyco is by and large known as a without a moment to spare (JIT) compiler. Psyco is in reality somewhat not the same as the JIT compilers a few perusers may have seen for the Java language, however. Truly, Psyco is a practicing JIT compiler it creates machine code customized to the information types that your program really employments. For instance, if a piece of your program utilizes distinctive information types at various occasions, Psyco may produce an alternate adaptation of machine code to help each extraordinary kind blend.

Psyco has been appeared to speed Python code significantly. As per its website page, Psyco gives "2x to 100x speed-ups, regularly 4x, with an unmodified Python translator and unmodified source code, simply a progressively loadable C expansion module." Of equivalent importance, the biggest speedups are acknowledged for algorithmic code written in unadulterated Python precisely such a code you may typically move to C to advance. With Psyco, such movements become even less significant.

Psyco isn't yet a standard piece of Python; you should get and introduce it independently. It is additionally as yet something of an exploration project, so you'll need to follow its development on the web. Indeed, at this composition, despite the fact that Psyco can in any case be gotten and introduced without anyone else, it creates the impression that a large part of the framework may ultimately be ingested into the more current "PyPy" project an endeavor to reimplement Python's PVM in Python code, to all the more likely help advancements like Psyco.

Maybe the biggest drawback of Psyco is that it right now just produces machine code for Intel x86 design chips, however this incorporates Windows and Linux boxes and ongoing Macs. For additional subtleties on the Psyco augmentation, and other JIT endeavors that may emerge, counsel site; you can likewise look at Psyco's landing page.

The Shedskin C++ translator: Shedskin is an arising framework that adopts an alternate strategy to Python program execution it endeavors to make an interpretation of Python source code to C++ code, which your PC's C++ compiler at that point assembles to machine code. Accordingly, it addresses a platform neutral way to deal with running Python code. Shedskin is still to some degree exploratory as I compose these words, and it limits Python projects to an understood statically composed limitation that is in fact not typical Python, so we will not broadly expound here.

Beginning outcomes, however, show that it can possibly beat both standard Python and the Psyco augmentation as far as execution speed, and it is a promising venture. Quest the Web for subtleties on the undertaking's present status.

2.3.3 Frozen Binaries

At times when individuals request a "genuine" Python compiler, what they're sincerely looking for is just an approach to produce independent double executable from their Python programs. This is more a bundling and delivery thought than an execution-stream idea, however it's to some degree related. With the assistance of outsider apparatuses that you can get off the Web, it is feasible to transform your Python programs into genuine executable, known as frozen pairs in the Python world.

Frozen parallels pack together the byte code of your program documents, alongside the PVM (mediator) and any Python support records your program needs, into a solitary bundle. There are a few minor departure from this topic, however the outcome can be a solitary paired executable program (e.g., an .exe record on Windows) that can undoubtedly be dispatched to clients. In Figure 2, it is like the byte code and PVM are converted into a single part a frozen parallel record.

Today, three essential frameworks are fit for creating frozen pairs: py2exe (for Windows), PyInstaller (which is like py2exe yet additionally chips away at Linux and Unix also, is fit for producing self-introducing parallels), and freeze (the first). You may need to bring these apparatuses independently from Python itself, however they are accessible for nothing out of pocket. They are additionally continually advancing, so counsel Python website or your #1 web internet searcher for additional on these instruments. To give you a thought of the extent of these frameworks, py2exe can freeze independent projects that utilization the tkinter, PMW, wxPython, and PyGTK GUI libraries; programs that utilization the pygame game programming tool compartment; win32com customer projects; and that's just the beginning.

Frozen pairs are not equivalent to the yield of a genuine compiler they run byte code through a virtual machine. Subsequently, aside from a potential startup improvement, frozen pairs run at a similar speed as the first source records. Frozen pairs are not little (they contain a PVM), but rather by current principles they are not surprisingly enormous all things considered.

Since Python is inserted in the frozen double, however, it doesn't need to be introduced on the less than desirable finish to run your program. Besides, in light of the fact that your code is inserted in the frozen parallel, it is all the more successfully stowed away from beneficiaries.

This single document bundling plan is particularly interesting to engineers of business programming. For example, a Python-coded UI program dependent on the tkinter tool stash can be frozen into an executable record and sent as an independent program on a CD or on the Web. End clients don't have to introduce (or even need to think about) Python to run the delivered program.

2.3.4 Other Execution Options

Then again different plans for running Python programs have more engaged objectives:

• The Stackless Python framework is a standard CPython execution variation that doesn't save state on the C language call stack. This makes Python all the more simple to port to little stack designs, gives productive multiprocessing choices, and encourages novel programming constructions.

• The Cython framework (in light of work done by the Pyrex project) is a half breed language that consolidates Python code with the capacity to call C capacities and utilize C sort presentations for factors, boundaries, and class ascribes. Cython code can be accumulated to C code that utilizes the Python/C API, which may then be assembled totally. In spite of the fact that not totally viable with standard Python, Cython can be valuable both for wrapping outside C libraries and for coding productive C expansions for Python.

For additional subtleties on these frameworks, scan the Web for late connections.

2.3.5 Future Possibilities?

At long last, note that the runtime execution model outlined here is actually an antique of the current execution of Python, not of the actual language. For example, it's certainly feasible that a full, conventional compiler for making an interpretation of Python source code to machine code may show up during the time span of usability of this book (albeit one has not in almost twenty years!). New byte code configurations and execution variations may likewise be embraced later on. For example:

• The Parrot project intends to give a typical byte code design, virtual machine, also, advancement methods for an assortment of programming dialects. Python's own PVM runs Python code more productively than Parrot, yet it's hazy how Parrot will advance.

• The PyPy project is an endeavor to implement again the PVM in Python itself to empower new execution methods. It will probably deliver a quick and adaptable execution of Python.

• The Google-supported Unladen Swallow project intends to make standard Python quicker by a factor of at any rate 5, and adequately quick to supplant the C language in numerous settings. It is a streamlining part of CPython, proposed to be completely viable what's more, altogether quicker. This task additionally desires to eliminate the Python multithreading Global Interpreter Lock (GIL), which forestalls unadulterated Python strings from genuinely covering on schedule. This is presently an arising project being created as open source by Google engineers; it is at first focusing on Python 2.6, however 3.0 may procure its progressions as well. Quest Google for forward-thinking subtleties.

Albeit such future execution plans may adjust the runtime construction of Python to some degree, it appears to be likely that the byte code compiler will in any case be the norm for quite a while to come. The movability and runtime adaptability of byte code are significant highlights of numerous Python frameworks. Also, adding type limitation affirmations to help static gathering would break the adaptability, succinctness, effortlessness, and in general soul of Python coding. Because of Python's exceptionally unique nature, any future execution will probably hold numerous curios of the current PVM.

Chapter 3. How You Run Programs

Alright, it's an ideal opportunity to begin running some code. Since you have an idea about program execution, you're at long last prepared to begin some genuine Python programming. Now, I'll expect that you have Python introduced on your PC; if not, see the earlier section and Appendix A for establishment and design hints.

There are an assortment of approaches to advise Python to execute the code you type. This section talks about all the program dispatching strategies in like manner use today. En route, you'll figure out how to type code intelligently and how to save it in records to be run with framework order lines, symbol clicks, module imports and reloads, executive calls, menu alternatives in GUIs like IDLE, and that's only the tip of the iceberg.

On the off chance that you simply need to discover how to run a Python program rapidly, you might be enticed to peruse the pieces of this part that relate just to your foundation and proceed onward to next Chapter. However, don't skirt the material on module imports, as that is crucial for understanding Python's program design. I likewise urge you to in any event skim the segments on IDLE and other IDEs, so you'll understand what apparatuses are accessible for when you begin growing more refined Python programs.

3.1 The Interactive Prompt

Maybe the least complex approach to run Python programs is to type them at Python's intuitive order line, now and then called the intelligent brief. There are an assortment of approaches to begin this order line: in an IDE, from a framework reassure, etc. Accepting the translator is introduced as an executable program on your framework, the most stage nonpartisan approach to begin an intelligent mediator meeting is normally to type python at your working framework's brief, with no contentions.

Composing "python" at your framework shell brief like this starts an intuitive Python meeting; the "%" character toward the beginning of this posting represents a nonexclusive framework brief in this book it's not information that you type yourself. The idea of a framework shell brief is conventional, yet precisely how you access it shifts by stage:

• On Windows, you can type python in a DOS support window (a.k.a. the Command Brief, generally found in the Accessories segment of the Start Programs menu) or in the Start Run exchange box.

• On UNIX, Linux, and Mac OS X, you may type this order in a shell or terminal window (e.g., in an xterm or support running a shell, for example, ksh or csh).

• Other frameworks may utilize comparative or stage explicit gadgets. On handheld gadgets, for instance, you by and large snap the Python symbol in the home or application window to dispatch an intuitive meeting.

On the off chance that you have not set your shell's PATH climate variable to incorporate Python's introduce registry, you may have to supplant "python" with the full way to the Python executable on your machine.

On the other hand, you can run a change-catalog order to go to Python's introduce registry prior to composing "python".

On Windows, other than composing python in a shell window, you can likewise start comparable intelligent meetings by beginning IDLE's fundamental window (examined later) or by choosing the "Python (order line)" menu alternative from the Start button menu for Python. Both produce a Python intuitive brief with comparable usefulness; composing a shell order isn't required.

3.1.1 Running Code Interactively

Anyway it's begun, the Python intuitive meeting starts by printing two lines of enlightening content (which I'll discard from the vast majority of this present book's guides to save space), at that point prompts for contribution with when it's sitting tight for you to type another Python proclamation or articulation. When working intelligently, the consequences of your code are shown after the lines after you press the Enter key.

For example, here are the consequences of two Python print proclamations (print is actually a work bring in Python 3.0, however not in 2.6, so the enclosures here are needed in 3.0 as it were).

Once more, you don't have to stress over the subtleties of the print explanations appeared here however; we'll begin delving into sentence structure in the following section. So, they print a Python string and a number, as demonstrated by the yield lines that show up after each info line.

When coding intuitively like this, you can type as numerous Python orders as you like; each is pursued quickly it's entered. Additionally, in light of the fact that the intuitive meeting naturally prints the consequences of articulations you type, you don't for the most part need to say "print" unequivocally at this brief.

Here, the clench hand line saves a worth by allocating it to a variable, and the last two lines composed are articulation, their outcomes are shown consequently. To leave an intuitive meeting like this one and get back to your framework shell brief, type Ctrl-D on Unix-like machines; on MS-DOS and Windows frameworks, type Ctrl-Z to exit.

In the IDLE GUI talked about later, either type Ctrl-D or basically close the window. Presently, we didn't do much in this current meeting's code just composed some Python print and task explanations, alongside a couple of articulations, which we'll concentrate in detail later. The primary concern to see is that the translator executes the code entered on each line promptly, when the Enter key is squeezed.

For instance, when we composed the main print explanation at the brief, the yield (a Python string) was repeated back immediately. There was no compelling reason to make a source code record, and no compelling reason to run the code through a compiler and linker first, as you'd ordinarily do when utilizing a language like C or C++. As you'll see in later sections, you can likewise run multiline articulations at the intelligent brief; such an explanation pursues promptly you've entered the entirety of its lines and squeezed Enter twice to add a clear line.

3.1.2 Why the Interactive Prompt?

The intuitive brief runs code and echoes results as you go, however it doesn't save your code in a record. Albeit this implies you will not do the heft of your coding in intelligent meetings, the intuitive brief ends up being an extraordinary spot to both investigation with the language and test program records on the fly.

Experimenting: Since code is executed quickly, the intelligent brief is an ideal spot to explore different avenues regarding the language and will be utilized regularly in this book to show more modest models. Indeed, this is the primary general guideline to recollect: in case you're ever in question about how a piece of Python code functions, fire up the intelligent order line and give it a shot to perceive what occurs.

For example, assume you're perusing a Python program's code and you run over an articulation like 'Spam!' whose significance you don't comprehend. Now, you can go through 10 minutes swimming through manuals and books to attempt to sort out what the code does, or you can basically run it intelligently.

The quick input you get at the intelligent brief is regularly the fastest method to reason what a piece of code does. Here, obviously it strings redundancy: in Python * implies increase for numbers, however rehash for strings it resembles linking a string to itself over and again.

Odds are acceptable that you will not break anything by testing this route at any rate, not yet. To do genuine harm, such as erasing documents and running shell orders, you should sincerely attempt, by bringing in modules unequivocally (you likewise need to find out about Python's framework interfaces overall before you will end up being that risky!). Straight Python code is quite often protected to run.

For example, watch what happens when you commit an error at the intuitive brief. In Python, utilizing a variable before it has been relegated a worth is consistently a mistake (in any case, if names were filled in with defaults, a few blunders may go undetected). We'll study that later; the significant point here is that you don't crash Python or your PC when you commit an error along these lines. All things being equal, you get a significant blunder message bringing up the error and the line of code that made it, and you can proceed in your meeting or content. Truth be told, when you get settled with Python, its blunder messages may frequently give as much troubleshooting support as you'll require (you'll read more on investigating in the sidebar).

Testing: Other than filling in as a device for testing while you're learning the language, the intuitive translator is additionally an ideal spot to test code you've written in documents. You can import your module records intelligently and run tests on the apparatuses they characterize by composing calls at the intuitive brief.

For example, of the accompanying tests a capacity in a pre-coded module that ships with Python in its standard library (it prints the name of the catalog you're presently working in), yet you can do the equivalent once you begin composing module records of your own.

All the more by and large, the intuitive brief is a spot to test program segments, paying little mind to their source you can import and test capacities and classes in your Python records, type calls to connected in C capacities, practice Java classes under Jython, and that's just the beginning. Somewhat on account of its intuitive nature, Python upholds a trial and exploratory programming style you'll discover helpful when beginning.

3.1.3 Using the Interactive Prompt

Albeit the intelligent brief is easy to use, there are a couple of tips that novices should remember. I'm including arrangements of basic missteps like this in this section for reference, however they may likewise save you from a couple of cerebral pains on the off chance that you read them in advance:

• Type Python orders as it were. Most importantly, recollect that you can just sort Python code at the Python fast, not framework orders. There are approaches to run framework orders from inside Python code (e.g., with OS framework), yet they are not as immediate as essentially composing the actual orders.

• Print proclamations are required distinctly in documents. Since the intuitive mediator consequently prints the consequences of articulations, you don't have to type total print proclamations intuitively. This is a pleasant component, however it will in general befuddle clients at the point when they proceed onward to composing code in records: inside a code document, you should utilize print proclamations to see yours.

• Don't indent at the intuitive brief (yet). When composing Python programs, either intuitively or into a book record, make certain to begin all your un-settled proclamations in section 1 (that is, right to one side). In the event that you don't, Python may print a "Linguistic structure Error" message, since clear space to one side of your code is taken to be space that gatherings settled explanations. Until Chapter 10, all proclamations you compose will be un-settled, so this incorporates everything for the time being. This is by all accounts a repeating disarray in starting Python classes. Keep in mind, a main space produces a mistake message.

• Watch out for brief changes for compound explanations. We will not meet compound (multiline) explanations until later section, however as a review, you should realize that when composing lines 2 and past of a compound assertion intuitively, the brief may change. In the straightforward shell window interface, the intuitive brief changes to dabs rather than prompts for lines 2 and past; in the IDLE interface, lines after the first are consequently indented.

Until further notice, in the event that you end up going over a brief or a clear line when entering your code, it most likely implies that you've by one way or another befuddled intuitive Python into believing you're composing a multiline explanation. Take a stab at hitting the Enter key or a Ctrl-C mix to return to the fundamental brief. The brief strings can likewise be transformed (they are accessible in the inherent module sys), yet I'll expect they have not been in the book's model postings.

• Terminate compound explanations at the intelligent brief with a clear line. At the intuitive brief, embedding a clear line (by hitting the Enter key at the beginning of a line) is important to tell intuitive Python that you're finished composing the multiline explanation. That is, you should press Enter twice to make a compound articulation run. Paradoxically, clear lines are not needed in records and are essentially overlooked if present. On the off chance that you don't press Enter twice toward the finish of a compound explanation when working intuitively, you'll give off an impression of being stuck in a limbo state, in light of the fact that the intelligent translator will do nothing by any stretch of the imagination it's hanging tight for you to press Enter once more!

• The intuitive brief runs each assertion in turn. At the intuitive brief, you should run one articulation to fruition prior to composing another. This is normal for basic explanations, since squeezing the Enter key runs the assertion entered.

For compound explanations, however, recall that you should present a clear line to end the assertion and make it run before you can type the following assertion.

Entering multiline statements: At the danger of rehashing the same thing, I got messages from per users who'd gotten scorched by the last two focuses as I was refreshing this section, so it most likely merits accentuation. I'll present multiline (a.k.a. compound) explanations in the following part, and we'll investigate their punctuation all the more officially later in this book. Since their conduct contrasts marginally in documents and at the intuitive brief, however, two alerts are all together here.

To start with, make certain to end multiline compound proclamations like for circles and if tests at the intelligent brief with a clear line. You should press the Enter key twice, to end the entire multiline proclamation and afterward make it run. For instance (play on words not proposed).

You needn't bother with the clear line after compound explanations in a content document, however; this is required distinctly at the intuitive brief. In a document, clear lines are not needed and are just overlooked when present; at the intelligent brief, they end multiline articulations.

Additionally remember that the intuitive brief runs only each proclamation in turn: you should press Enter twice to run a circle or other multiline proclamation before you can type the following assertion.

This implies you can't reorder numerous lines of code into the intelligent brief, except if the code incorporates clear lines after each compound proclamation. Such code is better disagreement a document the following areas subject.

3.2 System Command Lines and Files

Albeit the intuitive brief is incredible for testing and testing, it has one major detriment: programs you type there disappear when the Python translator executes them. Since the code you type intelligently is never put away in a document, you can't run it again without retyping it without any preparation. Reorder and order review can help some here, however very little, particularly when you begin composing bigger projects. To reorder code from an intelligent meeting, you would need to alter out Python prompts, program yields, etc. not by and large a cutting edge programming advancement system.

To save programs for all time, you need to compose your code in documents, which are generally known as modules. Modules are basically text records containing Python explanations. Once coded, you can request that the Python translator execute the assertions in such a document quite a few times, and in an assortment of ways by framework order lines, by record symbol clicks, by choices in the IDLE UI, and the sky is the limit from there. Notwithstanding how it is run, Python executes all the code in a module document start to finish each time you run the record.

Wording in this area can fluctuate to some degree. For example, module documents are regularly alluded to as projects in Python that is, a program is viewed as a progression of pre coded proclamations put away in a document for rehashed execution. Module records that are run straightforwardly are additionally now and then called contents a casual term generally meaning a high level program document. Some save the expression "module" for a record imported from another document.

(More on the significance of "high level" and imports in no time flat.) Whatever you call them, the following not many segments investigate approaches to run code composed into module records. In this segment, you'll figure out how to run documents in the most fundamental manner: by posting their names in a python order line entered at your PC's framework brief. Despite the fact that it may appear to be crude to a few, for some software engineers a framework shell order line window, along with word processor window, comprises as a lot of a coordinated advancement climate as they will at any point need.

3.2.1 A First Script

How about we begin. Open your #1 word processor (e.g., Notepad, or the IDLE supervisor), also, type the accompanying assertions into another content document named script1.py.

This record is our first authority Python content. You shouldn't stress a lot over this present document's code, however as a short depiction, this record:

• Imports a Python module (libraries of extra devices), to get the name of the stage.

• Runs three print work calls, to show the content's outcomes.

• Uses a variable named x, made when it's relegated, to clutch a string object.

• Applies different item tasks that we'll start concentrating in the following part.

The sys.platform here is only a string that distinguishes the sort of PC you're dealing with; it lives in a standard Python module called sys, which you should import to stack (once more, more on imports later).

For shading, I've likewise added some conventional Python remarks here the content after the # characters. Remarks can appear on lines without help from anyone else, or to one side of code on a line. The content after a # is just overlooked as a comprehensible remark and isn't viewed as a feature of the assertion's punctuation. In case you're replicating this code, you can disregard the remarks also. In this book, we ordinarily utilize an alternate arranging style to offer remarks all the more outwardly unmistakable, yet they'll show up as would be expected content in your code.

Once more, don't zero in on the linguistic structure of the code in this document for the present; we'll find out pretty much all of it later. The central matter to see is that you've composed this code into a document, instead of at the intuitive brief. All the while, you've coded a completely practical Python content.

Notice that the module document is called script1.py. Concerning all high level records, it could likewise be called just content, however documents of code you need to bring into a customer need to end with a .py addition. We'll consider imports later in this section. Since you might need to import them later on, it's a smart thought to utilize .py postfixes for most Python records that you code. Additionally, some content tools identify Python records by their .py postfix; if the addition is absent, you may not get highlights like sentence structure colorization and programmed space.

Conclusion

Also, that closes the publicity bit of this book. In this part, we've investigated a portion of the reasons that individuals pick Python for their programming errands. We've additionally perceived how it is applied and taken a gander at an agent test of who is utilizing it today. I will likely show Python, however, not to sell it. The most ideal approach to pass judgment on a language is to see it in real life, so the remainder of this book centers altogether on the language subtleties we've overlooked here.

In this book, we'll investigate approaches to run Python programs, look at Python's byte code execution model, and present the fundamentals of module documents for saving code. The objective will be to give you barely enough data to run the models and activities in the remainder of the book. You will not actually begin programming, yet ensure you have an idea about the startup subtleties prior to proceeding onward.

PYTHON
PROGRAMMING

A Complete Guide For Beginners to Learn Python Programming and Becoming an Expert in Programming.

BY JOHN BROWN

© Copyright 2021 by - All rights reserved.

This document is geared towards providing exact and reliable information in regards to the topic and issue covered. The publication is sold with the idea that the publisher is not required to render accounting, officially permitted, or otherwise, qualified services. If advice is necessary, legal or professional, a practiced individual in the profession should be ordered.

- From a Declaration of Principles which was accepted and approved equally by a Committee of the American Bar Association and a Committee of Publishers and Associations.

In no way is it legal to reproduce, duplicate, or transmit any part of this document in either electronic means or in printed format. Recording of this publication is strictly prohibited and any storage of this document is not allowed unless with written permission from the publisher. All rights reserved.

The information provided herein is stated to be truthful and consistent, in that any liability, in terms of inattention or otherwise, by any usage or abuse of any policies, processes, or directions contained within is the solitary and utter responsibility of the recipient reader. Under no circumstances will any legal responsibility or blame be held against the publisher for any reparation, damages, or monetary loss due to the information herein, either directly or indirectly.

Respective authors own all copyrights not held by the publisher.

The information herein is offered for informational purposes solely and is universal as such. The presentation of the information is without a contract or any type of guarantee assurance.

The trademarks that are used are without any consent, and the publication of the trademark is without permission or backing by the trademark owner. All trademarks and brands within this book are for clarifying purposes only and are owned by the owners themselves, not affiliated with this document.

Chapter 1. Running Files with Command Lines in Python

Whenever you've saved this content document, you can request that Python show it to posting its full filename as the primary contention to a python order, composed at the framework shell brief.

Once more, you can type such a framework shell order in whatever your framework gives for order line passage a Windows Command Prompt window, a x-term window, or then again comparable. Make sure to supplant "python" with a full registry way, as in the past, if your way setting isn't designed.

On the off chance that all fills in as arranged, this shell order makes Python run the code in this document line by line, and you will see the yield of the content's three print explanations the name of the fundamental stage, 2 raised to the force 100, and the aftereffect of a similar string reiteration articulation we saw before.

In the event that all didn't fill in as arranged, you'll get a mistake message ensure you've entered the code in your record precisely as appeared, and attempt once more. We'll discuss troubleshooting choices in the sidebar, however now in the book your smartest choice is presumably repetition impersonation.

Since this plan utilizes shell order lines to begin Python programs, all the typical shell linguistic structure applies. For example, you can course the yield of a Python content to a record to save it for some time in the future or assessment by utilizing unique shell language structure: For this situation, the three yield lines appeared in the earlier run are put away in the document saveit.txt as opposed to being printed. This is by and large known as stream redirection; it works for information and yield text and is accessible on Windows and Unix-like frameworks. It additionally has little to do with (Python essentially upholds it), so we will skirt further subtleties on shell redirection sentence structure here.

Of course, make certain to type the full way to Python on the off chance that you haven't set your PATH climate variable to incorporate this way or run a change-registry order to go to the way. On all new forms of

Windows, you can likewise type simply the name of your content, and exclude the name of Python itself. Since fresher Windows frameworks utilize the Windows Vault to discover a program with which to run a record, you don't have to name "python" on the order line unequivocally to run document. The earlier order, for instance, could be streamlined to this on most Windows machines.

At last, make sure to give the full way to your content document on the off chance that it lives in an alternate index from the one in which you are working. For instance, the accompanying framework order line, run from D:\other, expects Python is in your framework way however runs a document found somewhere else.

In the event that your PATH does exclude Python's catalog, and neither Python nor your content record is in the registry you're working in, utilize full ways for both.

1.1 Using Command Lines and Files

Running project records from framework order lines is likewise a genuinely clear dispatch choice, particularly on the off chance that you know about order lines overall from earlier work. For rookies, however, here are a couple of pointers about basic fledgling snares that may assist you with keeping away from dissatisfaction:

• Beware of programmed augmentations on Windows. In the event that you utilize the Notepad program to code program documents on Windows, be mindful so as to pick the sort All Files when it comes time to save your document, and give the record a postfix unequivocally. Something else, Notebook will save your document with a .txt expansion, making it hard to run in some starting plans.

More awful, Windows conceals record augmentations of course, so except if you have changed your see choices you may not notification that you've coded a content document and not a Python record. The document's symbol may give this on the off chance that it doesn't have a snake on it, you may experience difficulty. Uncolored code in IDLE and documents that open to alter rather than run when clicked are different manifestations of this issue.

Microsoft Word likewise adds a .doc expansion as a matter of course; much more awful, it adds designing characters that are not lawful Python sentence structure. As a dependable guideline, consistently pick All Files when saving under Windows, or utilize a more developer agreeable content manager like IDLE. Inactive doesn't add a postfix consequently a include developers will in general like, however clients don't.

• Use document expansions and registry ways at framework prompts, however not for imports. Remember to type the complete name of your record in framework order lines that is, use python script1.py instead of python script1. Conversely, Python's import proclamations, which we'll meet later in this part, preclude both the record postfix and the registry way. This may appear to be unimportant, however befuddling these two is a typical slip up.

At the framework brief, you are in a framework shell, not Python, so Python's module document search rules don't have any significant bearing. Thus, you should incorporate both the expansion and, if fundamental, the full registry way prompting the record you wish to run. For example, to run a document that dwells in an alternate catalog from the one in which you are working, you would normally list its full way. Inside Python code, be that as it may, you can simply say import spam and depend on the Python module search way to find your document, as portrayed later.

• Use print articulations in documents. Indeed, we've effectively been over this, however it is such a normal mix-up that it merits rehashing at any rate once here. Dissimilar to in intelligent coding, you by and large should utilize print explanations to see yield from program documents. On the off chance that you don't perceive any yield, ensure you've said "print" in your record. Once more, however, print articulations are not needed in an intuitive meeting, since Python consequently echoes articulation results; prints don't hurt here, however are unnecessary additional composing.

1.2 UNIX Executable Scripts

In the event that you will utilize Python on a UNIX, Linux, or Unix-like framework, you can likewise transform records of Python code into executable projects, much as you would for programs coded in a shell language. Such records are normally called executable contents. In basic terms, Unix-style executable contents are simply ordinary content records containing Python proclamations, however with two uncommon properties:

• Their first line is exceptional. Contents generally start with a line that starts with the characters (Regularly called "hash bang"), trailed by the way to the Python translator on your machine.

• They normally have executable advantages. Content documents are typically set apart as executable to tell the working framework that they might be run as high level projects. On UNIX frameworks, an order, normally gets the job done.

The unique line at the highest point of the record tells the framework where the Python mediator resides. In fact, the main line is a Python remark. As referenced before, all remarks in

Python programs start with and length to the furthest limit of the line; they are a spot to embed additional data for human per users of your code. In any case, when a remark, for example, the main line in this document shows up, it's exceptional on the grounds that the working framework utilizes it to discover a mediator for running the program code in the remainder of the record.

Likewise, note that this document is called, without the addition utilized for the module record prior. Adding to the name wouldn't do any harm (and may assist you with recalling that this is a Python program document), but since you don't anticipate allowing different modules to import the code in this record, the name of the record is immaterial. In the event that you give the record executable advantages with a shell order, you can run it from the working framework shell like it were a twofold program.

A note for Windows clients: the strategy portrayed here is a UNIX stunt, and it may not work on your foundation. Not to stress; simply utilize the essential order line method investigated before. Rundown the record's name on an unequivocal python order line.

As we talked about when investigating order lines, present day Windows forms likewise let you type simply the name of a document at the framework order line they utilize the Registry to establish that the record ought to be opened with Python (e.g., composing brian.py is identical to composing python brian.py). This order line mode is comparative in soul to the UNIX, however it is framework wide on Windows, not per record. Note that a few projects may really decipher and utilize a first line on Windows similar as on UNIX, yet the DOS framework shell on Windows just disregards it.

For this situation, you needn't bother with the uncommon remark at the top (in spite of the fact that Python just overlooks it if it's present), and the document shouldn't be given executable advantages. Indeed, on the off chance that you need to run documents transportable among UNIX and Microsoft Windows, your life will most likely be less difficult in the event that you generally utilize the essential order line approach, not UNIX style contents, to dispatch programs.

At the point when coded along these lines, the program finds the Python mediator as per your framework search way settings (i.e., in most UNIX shells, by glancing in every one of the indexes recorded in the PATH climate variable). This plan can be more versatile, as you don't have to hardcode a Python introduce way in the main line of every one of your contents.

If you approach all over, your contents will run regardless of where Python lives on your framework you need just change the PATH climate variable settings across stages, not in the principal line in the entirety of your contents. Obviously, this accepts that lives in a similar spot all over the place (on certain machines, it could be somewhere else); if not, all transportability wagers are off!

1.3 Clicking File Icons

On Windows, the Registry makes opening records with symbol clicks simple. Python automatically enrolls itself to be the program that opens Python program documents when they are clicked. Thus, it is feasible to dispatch the Python programs you compose by basically clicking (or double tapping) on their document symbols with your mouse cursor. On non-Windows frameworks, you can likely play out a comparable stunt, yet the symbols, document pioneer, route plans, and more may contrast marginally. On a few UNIX frameworks, for example, you may have to enlist the augmentation with your record adventurer GUI, make your content executable utilizing the stunt examined in the past segment, or partner the record MIME type with an application or order by altering records, introducing projects, or utilizing different devices. See your record traveler's documentation for additional subtleties if clicks don't work accurately first thing.

1.3.1 Clicking Icons on Windows

To outline, how about we continue to utilize the content we composed before, rehashed here to limit page flipping. Nonetheless, symbol clicks permit you to run the document with no composing by any means. On the off chance that you discover this document's symbol for example, by choosing Computer (or My Computer in XP) in your Start menu and working your way down on the C drive on Windows you will get the document pioneer picture caught in Figure 1 (Windows Vista is being utilized here). Python source documents appear with white foundations on Windows, and byte code records show up with dark foundations. You will ordinarily need to click (or in any case run) the source code record, to get your latest changes. To dispatch the document here, essentially click on the symbol for script1.py.

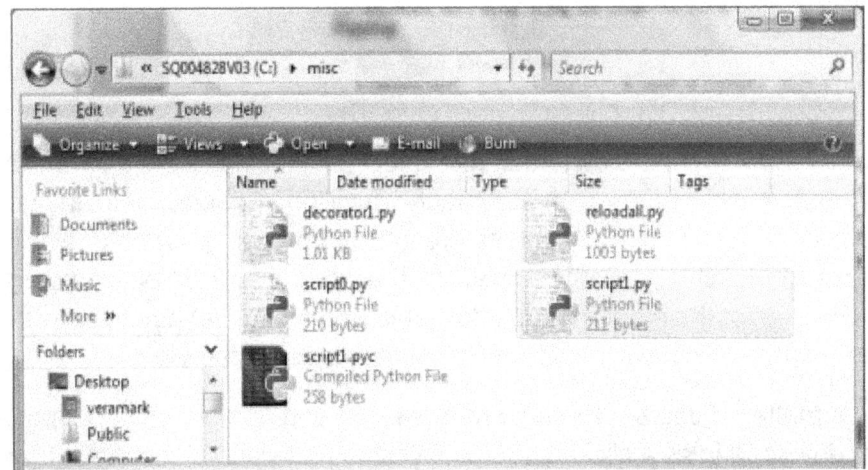

Figure 1: On Windows, Python program records appear as symbols in document wayfarer windows and can consequently be run with a double tap of the mouse.

1.3.2 The input Trick

Lamentably, on Windows, the aftereffect of tapping on a document symbol may not be unfathomably fulfilling. Indeed, all things considered, this model content creates a confusing "streak" when clicked not actually such a criticism that sprouting Python software engineers for the most part trust for! This isn't a bug, yet has to do with the way the Windows variant of Python handles printed yield.

As a matter of course, Python produces a spring up dark DOS support window to fill in as a clicked document's info and yield. In the event that a content simply prints and leaves, indeed, it simply prints and leaves the reassure window shows up, and text is printed there, however the support window closes and vanishes on program exit. Except if you are quick, or your machine is exceptionally sluggish, you will not will see your yield by any means. Albeit this is typical conduct, it's presumably not what you had as a primary concern.

Fortunately, it's not difficult to work around this. On the off chance that you need your content's yield to stay at the point when you dispatch it with a symbol click, just put a call to the implicit info work at the actual lower part of the content.

By and large, input peruses the following line of standard info, pausing if there is none yet accessible. The net impact in this setting will be to stop the content, subsequently keeping the yield window appeared in Figure 2 open until you press the Enter key.

Figure 2: *At the point when you click a program's symbol on Windows, you will actually want to see its printed yield in the event that you incorporate an info call at the finish of the content. Yet, you just need to do as such in this unique circumstance!*

Since I've shown you this stunt, remember that it is generally just needed for Windows, and afterward just if your content prints text and exits and just in the event that you will dispatch the content by clicking its document symbol. You should add this call to the lower part of your high level documents if and just if these three conditions apply. There is no motivation to add this bring in some other settings (except if you're irrationally attached to squeezing your figure's Enter key!). That may sound self-evident, however it's another regular slip-up in live classes.

Before we push forward, note that the information call applied here is the information partner of utilizing the print proclamation for yields. It is the most straightforward approach to peruse client info, and it is broader than this model infers. For example, input.

1.3.3 Other Icon Click Limitations

Indeed, even with the info stunt, clicking document symbols isn't without its risks. You additionally may not will see Python blunder messages. In the event that your content produces a mistake, the blunder message text is kept in touch with the spring up reassure window which at that point promptly vanishes! More awful, adding an info call to your record won't help this time on the grounds that your content will probably cut short well before it arrives at this call. All in all, you will not have the option to determine what turned out badly.

It is likewise conceivable to totally smother the spring up DOS comfort window for clicked documents on Windows. Documents whose names end in augmentation will show just windows built by your content, not the default DOS reassure window documents are basically source records that have this exceptional operational conduct on Windows. They are generally utilized for Python-coded UIs that form windows of their own, frequently related to different strategies for saving printed yield and blunders to records.

As a result of these restrictions, it is likely best to see symbol clicks as an approach to dispatch programs after they have been fixed or have been instrumented to compose their yield to a document. Particularly when beginning, utilize different procedures like framework order lines and IDLE (talked about further in the part so you can see produced mistake messages and view your typical yield without falling back on coding stunts. At the point when we examine special cases later in this book, you'll additionally discover that it is feasible to catch and recuperate from blunders so they don't end your projects. Watch for the conversation of the attempt explanation later in this book for an elective method to hold the reassure window back from shutting on mistakes.

1.4 Module Imports and Reloads

Up until now, I've been looking at "bringing in modules" without truly clarifying what this term implies. We'll contemplate modules and bigger program engineering top to bottom, but since imports are likewise an approach to dispatch programs, this part will present enough module rudiments to kick you off.

In basic terms, each record of Python source code whose name closes in an expansion is a module. Different records can get to the things a module characterizes by bringing in that module; import activities basically load another document and award admittance to that record's substance.

The substance of a module are made accessible to the rest of the world through it ascribes (a term I'll characterize in the following segment). This module-based administrations model ends up being the center thought behind program design in Python. Bigger projects typically appear as various module documents, which import devices from other module documents. One of the modules is assigned as the primary or high level document, and this is the one dispatched to begin the whole program.

We'll dig into such compositional issues in more detail later in this book. This section is generally inspired by the way that import activities run the code in a document that is being stacked as a last advance. Along these lines, bringing in a document is one more approach to dispatch it.

For example, in the event that you start an intuitive meeting (from a framework order line, from the Start menu, from IDLE, or else), you can run the script1.py document you made before with a basic import (make certain to erase the information line you included the earlier area first, or you'll have to press Enter for reasons unknown).

This works, however just once per meeting (truly, measure) as a matter of course. After the principal import, later imports sit idle, regardless of whether you change and save the module's source record again in another window:

This is by configuration; imports are too costly an activity to rehash more than once per document, per program run, imports should discover records, arrange them to byte code, and run the code.

On the off chance that you truly need to compel Python to run the record again in a similar meeting without halting and restarting the meeting, you need to rather call the reload work accessible in the devil standard library module (this capacity is likewise a basic implicit in Python.

From proclamation here just duplicates a name out of a module (more on this soon). The reload work itself loads and runs the current form of your record's code, getting changes on the off chance that you've changed and saved it in another window.

This permits you to alter and get new code on the fly inside the current Python intelligent meeting. In this meeting, for instance, the second print explanation in script1.py was changed in another window to print between the hour of the first import and the reload call.

The reload work expects the name of a generally stacked module object, so you must have effectively imported a module once before you reload it. Notice that reload additionally expects enclosures around the module object name, while import doesn't reload is a capacity that is called, and import is an assertion.

That is the reason you should pass the module name to reload as a contention in brackets, and that is the reason you get back an additional yield line while reloading. The last yield line is only the showcase portrayal of the reload call's return esteem, a Python module object. We'll become familiar with utilizing capacities as a rule.

1.4.1 The Grander Module Story: Attributes

Imports and reloads give a characteristic program dispatch choice since import activities execute records as a last advance. In the more extensive plan of things, however, modules serve the job of libraries of devices, as you'll learn later. All the more by and large, a module is generally a bundle of variable names, known as a namespace. The names inside that bundle are considered credits a trait is just a variable name that is connected to a particular article (like a module).

In average use, shippers access every one of the names appointed at the high level of a module's document. These names are normally allocated to instruments traded by the module capacities, classes, factors, etc. that are proposed to be utilized in different documents and different projects. Remotely, a module document's names can be brought with two Python proclamations, import and from, just as the reload call.

To delineate, utilize a content tool to make a one-line Python module document called myfile.py with the accompanying substance. This might be one of the world's most straightforward Python modules (it contains a solitary task articulation), yet it's sufficient to delineate the point. At the point when this document is imported, its code is raced to produce the module's characteristic. The task proclamation makes a module property named title.

You can get to this present module's title characteristic in different segments in two distinct ways. In the first place, you can stack the module all in all with an import proclamation, and afterward qualify the module name with the characteristic name to get it.

All in all, the dab articulation grammar object attribute allows you to get any characteristic appended to any object, and this is a typical activity in Python code. Here, we've utilized it to get to the string variable title inside the module my file in other words, my file title.

As you'll find in more detail later, from is actually similar to an import, with an additional task to names in the bringing in segment. Actually, from duplicates a module's credits, to such an extent that they become straightforward factors in the beneficiary along these lines, you can essentially allude to the imported string this time as title (a variable) rather than my file title (a trait reference).

Regardless of whether you use import or from to summon an import activity, the assertions in the module record myfile.py are executed, and the bringing in segment (here, the intuitive brief) accesses names doled out at the high level of the document. There's just one such name in this basic model the variable title, allotted to a string however the idea will be more valuable when you begin characterizing articles like capacities and classes in your modules: such items become reusable programming parts that can be gotten to by name from at least one customer modules.

This record, threenames.py, allots three factors, thus produces three credits for the rest of the world. It likewise utilizes its own three factors in a print proclamation, as we see at the point when we run this as a high level document:

Notice that import and from both rundown the name of the module document as basically my file without its postfix. As you'll learn in Part V, when Python searches for the genuine record, it knows to remember the postfix for its hunt method. Once more, you should incorporate the addition in framework shell order lines, yet not in import explanations.

The entirety of this current document's code runs as regular the first occasion when it is imported somewhere else (by one or the other an import or from). Customers of this document that utilization import get a module with credits, while customers that utilization from get duplicates of the record's names.

The outcomes here are imprinted in brackets since they are truly tuples (a sort of object shrouded in the following piece of this book); you can securely disregard them for the time being. When you begin coding modules with various names this way, the implicit work begins to prove to be useful you can utilize it to get a rundown of the names accessible inside a module. The accompanying returns a Python rundown of strings.

I ran this on new Python renditions, more seasoned Pythons may return less names. At the point when the work is called with the name of an imported module passed in brackets this way, it returns every one of the credits inside that module. A portion of the names it returns are names you get "free of charge": names with driving and following twofold underscores are implicit names that are consistently predefined by Python and that have unique significance to the mediator. The factors our code characterized by task a, b, and c appear rearward in the result.

Modules and namespaces: Module imports are an approach to run documents of code, yet, as we'll talk about later in the book, modules are additionally the biggest program structure in Python programs.

When all is said in done, Python programs are made out of numerous module records, connected together by import proclamations. Every module document is an independent bundle of factors that is, a namespace. One module document can't see the names characterized in another record except if it expressly imports that other record, so modules serve to limit name impacts in your code on the grounds that each document is an independent namespace, the names in a single document can't conflict with those in another, regardless of whether they are spelled a similar way.

Indeed, as you'll see, modules are one of a modest bunch of ways that Python goes to incredible lengths to bundle your factors into compartments to keep away from name conflicts. We'll talk about modules and other namespace develops (counting classes and capacity scopes) further later in the book. For the time being, modules will prove to be useful as an approach to run your code ordinarily without having to retype it.

1.4.2 Import and reload Usage Notes

For reasons unknown, when individuals get some answers concerning running documents utilizing import and reload, many will in general zero in on this by itself and disregard other dispatch alternatives that consistently run the current variant of the code (e.g., symbol clicks, IDLE menu alternatives, and framework order lines). This methodology can rapidly prompt disarray, however you need to recall when you've imported to know whether you can reload, you need to make sure to utilize brackets when you call reload (just), and you need to make sure to utilize reload in any case to get the current adaptation of your code to run. Besides, reloads aren't transitive reloading a module reloads that module just, no modules it might import so you here and there need to reload different records.

Due to these confusions (and others we'll investigate later, including the reload/ from issue referenced in an earlier note in this part), it's by and large a smart thought to keep away from the compulsion to dispatch by imports and reloads until further notice. The IDLE Run Module menu choice portrayed in the following segment, for instance, gives a less difficult and less mistake inclined approach to run your records, and consistently runs the current adaptation of your code.

Framework shell order lines offer comparable advantages. You don't have to utilize reload in the event that you utilize these strategies.

What's more, you may run into inconvenience in the event that you use modules in strange manners now in the book. For example, on the off chance that you need to import a module document that is put away in a registry other than the one you're working and find out about the module search way.

For the time being, on the off chance that you should import, attempt to keep every one of your records in the registry you are working in to keep away from difficulties.

All things considered, imports and reloads have demonstrated to be a famous testing method in Python classes, and you may incline toward utilizing this methodology as well. Not surprisingly, however, on the off chance that you end up running into a divider, quit running into a divider!

1.5 Using exec to Run Module Files

Indeed, there are more approaches to run code put away in module documents than have yet been uncovered here. For example, the inherent capacity call is another approach to dispatch documents from the intelligent brief without bringing in and later reload. Every executive runs the current rendition of the record, without requiring later reloads.

The executive call has an impact like an import, yet it doesn't actually import the module naturally, each time you call executive this way it runs the document over again, like you had glued it in at where executive is called. Hence, executive doesn't require module reloads after record transforms it avoids the ordinary module import rationale.

On the disadvantage, since it fills in as though gluing code into where it is called, executive, similar to the from articulation referenced before, can possibly quietly overwrite factors you may at present be utilizing. For instance, our script1.py allocates to a variable named x. In the event that that name is likewise being utilized in where executive is called, the name's worth is supplanted.

If you're igniting with interest, the short story is that Python looks for imported modules in each catalog recorded in Python rundown of index name strings in the sys module, which is introduced from a PYTHONPATH climate variable, in addition to a bunch of standard registries. On the off chance that you need to import from a catalog other than the one you are working in, that registry should for the most part be recorded in your PYTHONPATH setting.

Conversely, the essential import proclamation runs the document just once per interaction, and it makes the record a different module namespace with the goal that its tasks won't change factors in your degree. The value you pay for the namespace apportioning of modules is the need to reload after changes.

1.6 The IDLE User Interface

Up until now, we've perceived how to run Python code with the intelligent brief, framework order lines, symbol snaps, and module imports and executive calls. In case you're searching for something a touch more visual, IDLE gives a graphical UI to doing Python advancement, and it's a norm and free piece of the Python framework. It is normally alluded to as an incorporated advancement climate (IDE), in light of the fact that it ties together different improvement undertakings into a solitary view.

So, IDLE is a GUI that allows you to alter, run, peruse, and troubleshoot Python programs, all from a solitary interface. Additionally, in light of the fact that IDLE is a Python program that utilizes the tkinter GUI tool compartment, it runs transportable on most Python stages, including Microsoft Windows, X Windows (for Linux, Unix, and Unix-like stages), and the Mac OS (both Classic and OS X). For some, IDLE addresses a simple to utilize option in contrast to composing order lines, and a less issue inclined option in contrast to tapping on symbols.

1.6.1 IDLE Basics

We should hop directly into a model. Inactive is not difficult to begin under Windows it has a passage in the Start button menu for Python, and it can likewise be chosen by right-tapping on a Python program symbol. On some UNIX like frameworks. Figure 3 shows the scene subsequent to beginning IDLE on Windows. The Python shell window that opens at first is the fundamental window, which runs an intuitive meeting (notice the brief). This works like all intelligent meetings code you type here is pursued promptly you type it and fills in as a testing apparatus.

```
Type "copyright", "credits" or "license()" for more information.
>>> 2 ** 100
1267650600228229401496703205376
>>> 'Spam!' * 15
'Spam!Spam!Spam!Spam!Spam!Spam!Spam!Spam!Spam!Spam!Spam!Spam!Spam!Spam!Spam!'
>>> X = 'Spam'
>>> X + 'NI'
'SpamNI'
>>> ================================ RESTART ================================
>>>
win32
1267650600228229401496703205376
Spam!Spam!Spam!Spam!Spam!Spam!Spam!Spam!
>>>
>>> import os
>>> os.getcwd()
'C:\\misc'
>>>
>>> import sys
>>> sys.platform
'win32'
>>> sys.path
['C:\\misc', 'C:\\Python31\\Lib\\idlelib', 'C:\\Windows\\system32\\python31.zip', 'C:\\
Python31\\DLLs', 'C:\\Python31\\lib', 'C:\\Python31\\lib\\plat-win', 'C:\\Python31', 'C
:\\Python31\\lib\\site-packages']
>>>
>>> help(bin)
Help on built-in function bin in module builtins:

bin(...)
    bin(number) -> string

    Return the binary representation of an integer or long integer.

>>> import this
```

Figure 3: The fundamental Python shell window of the IDLE advancement GUI, appeared here running on Windows.

Inactive is a Python program that utilizes the standard library's tkinter GUI tool compartment to assemble the IDLE GUI. This makes IDLE compact, yet it additionally implies that you'll have to have tkinter support in your Python to utilize IDLE. The Windows form of Python has this naturally, yet some Linux and Unix clients may have to introduce the proper tkinter support (a yum tkinter order may get the job done on some Linux appropriations, however see the establishment hints in Appendix A for subtleties). Macintosh OS X may have all that you need preinstalled, as well; search for an inactive order or content on your machine.

Inactive utilizations comfortable menus with console easy routes for the greater part of its tasks. To make (or on the other hand alter) a source code record under IDLE, open a content alter window: in the primary window, select the File pull-down menu, and pick New Window (or Open... to open a content alter window showing a current document for altering).

Despite the fact that it may not appear completely in this current book's designs, IDLE uses sentence structure coordinated colorization for the code composed in both the fundamental window and all content alter windows catchphrases are one tone, literals are another, etc. This aides give you a superior image of the segments in your code (and can even assistance you spot botches run on strings are each of the one tone, for instance).

To run a record of code that you are altering in IDLE, select the document's content alter window, open that window's Run pull-down menu, and pick the Run Module alternative recorded there (or utilize the same console alternate way, given in the menu). Python will tell you that you need to save your document first in the event that you've transformed it since it was opened or last saved and neglected to save your progressions a typical error when you're knee somewhere down in coding.

At the point when run thusly, the yield of your content and any blunder messages it might produce appear back in the fundamental intelligent window (the Python shell window). In Figure 3, for instance, the three lines after the "RESTART" line close to the center of the window mirror an execution of our script1.py record opened in a different alter window. The "RESTART" message discloses to us that the client code measure was restarted to run the altered content and serves to isolate content yield (it doesn't show up if IDLE is begun without a client code sub interaction more on this mode in a second).

If you need to rehash earlier orders in IDLE's primary intuitive window, you can utilize the Alt-P key blend to scroll in reverse through the order history, and Alt-N to look forward (on certain Macs, attempt Ctrl-P and Ctrl-N all things being equal). Your earlier orders will be reviewed and shown, and might be altered and rerun. You can likewise review orders by situating the cursor on them, or utilize reorder tasks, however these methods will in general include more work. Outside IDLE, you might have the option to review orders in an intuitive meeting with the bolt keys on Windows.

1.6.2 Using IDLE

Inactive is free, simple to utilize, versatile, and naturally accessible on most stages. I by and large prescribe it to Python novices since it glosses over a portion of the subtleties and doesn't accept related knowledge with framework order lines. Be that as it may, it is to some degree restricted contrasted with further developed business IDEs. To assist you with keeping away from normal traps, here is a rundown of issues that IDLE novices should remember:

• You should add expressly when saving your documents. I referenced this when discussing documents as a rule, yet it's a typical IDLE hindrance, particularly for Windows clients. Inactive doesn't naturally add expansion to filenames at the point when records are saved. Be mindful so as to type the augmentation yourself when saving a record interestingly. In the event that you don't, while you will actually want to run your record from IDLE (what's more, framework order lines), you won't import it either intelligently or then again from different modules.

• Run contents by choosing Run Module in text alter windows, not by intelligent imports and reloads. Prior in this part, we saw that it's conceivable to show a document to bringing in it intuitively. Notwithstanding, this plan can develop complex since it expects you to physically reload records after changes. Paradoxically, utilizing the Run Module menu choice in IDLE consistently runs the most current rendition of your document, very much like running it utilizing a framework shell order line. Inactive too prompts you to save your record first, if necessary (another basic error outside Inactive).

• You need to reload just modules being tried intuitively. Like framework shell order lines, IDLE's Run Module menu choice consistently runs the current adaptation of both the high level document and any modules it imports. Along these lines, Run Module disposes of normal disarrays encompassing imports. You as it were need to reload modules that you are bringing in and testing intelligently in IDLE.

In the event that you decide to utilize the import and reload procedure rather than Run Module, recollect that you can utilize the Alt-P/Alt-N key mixes to review earlier orders.

• You can modify IDLE. To change the content textual styles and tones in IDLE, select the Design alternative in the Options menu of any IDLE window. You can likewise alter key blend activities, space settings, and then some; see IDLE's Help pull-down menu for additional clues.

• There is right now no reasonable screen alternative in IDLE. This is by all accounts a continuous demand (maybe in light of the fact that it's an alternative accessible in comparable IDEs), and it very well may be added in the end. Today, however, it is extremely unlikely to clear the intuitive window's text. In the event that you need the window's content to disappear, you can either press and hold the Enter key, or type a Python circle to print a progression of clear lines (no one truly employments the last method, obviously, yet it sounds more cutting edge than squeezing the Enter key!).

- tkinter GUI and strung projects may not function admirably with IDLE. Since Inactive is a Python/tkinter program, it can hang in the event that you use it to run specific kinds of progressed Python/tkinter programs. This has gotten less of an issue in later forms of IDLE that run client code in one cycle and the IDLE GUI itself in another, yet a few projects (particularly those that utilization multithreading) may in any case hang the GUI. Your code may not show such issues, however as a general guideline, it's consistently protected to utilize IDLE to alter GUI programs however dispatch them utilizing other choices, for example, symbol snaps or framework order lines. If all else fails, if your code fizzles in IDLE, attempt it outside the GUI.

- If association mistakes emerge, have a go at beginning IDLE in single-measure mode. Since Inactive requires correspondence between its different client and GUI measures, it can some of the time experience difficulty firing up on specific stages (remarkably, it neglects to begin incidentally on certain Windows machines, because of firewall programming that blocks associations). In the event that you run into such association mistakes, it's consistently conceivable to begin Inactive with a framework order line that drives it to run in single measure mode without a client code sub interaction and in this way stays away from correspondence issues: it order line banner powers this mode. On Windows, for instance, start a Command Prompt window and run the framework order line from inside the registry.

- Beware of some IDLE convenience highlights. Inactive does a lot to make life simpler for novices, yet a portion of its stunts will not make a difference outside the IDLE GUI. For example, IDLE runs your contents in its own intelligent namespace, so factors in your code appear consequently in the IDLE intuitive meeting you don't generally have to run import orders to get to names at the high degree of documents you've as of now run. This can be helpful, however it can likewise be confounding, on the grounds that external the Inactive climate names should consistently be imported from records to be utilized.

Inactive additionally naturally changes both to the index of a record just run and adds its catalog to the module import search way a helpful element that permits you to import records there without search way settings, yet in addition something that will not work a similar when you run documents outside IDLE. It's OK to utilize such highlights, yet remember that they are IDLE conduct, not Python conduct.

1.6.3 Advanced IDLE Tools

Other than the fundamental alter and run capacities, IDLE gives further developed highlights, including a point-and-snap program debugger and an item program. The IDLE debugger is empowered through the Debug menu and the item program by means of the File menu. The program permits you to explore through the module search way to records and items in documents; tapping on a record or article opens the comparing source in a content alter window.

Inactive troubleshooting is started by choosing the Debugger menu alternative in the principle window and afterward beginning your content by choosing the Run Module choice in the text alter window; when the debugger is empowered, you can set breakpoints in your code that stop its execution by right-tapping on lines in the content alter windows, show variable qualities, etc. You can likewise watch program execution while investigating the current line of code is noted as you venture through your code.

For less difficult troubleshooting activities, you can likewise right-click with your mouse on the content of a blunder message to rapidly leap to the line of code where the mistake happened a stunt that simplifies it and quick to fix and run once more. Likewise, IDLE's content supervisor offers a huge assortment of developer agreeable devices, including programmed space, progressed text and record search tasks, and the sky is the limit from there. Since IDLE uses natural GUI associations, you should explore different avenues regarding the framework live to figure out its different devices.

1.7 Other IDEs

Since IDLE is free, versatile, and a standard piece of Python, it's a decent first improvement instrument to get comfortable with in the event that you need to utilize an IDE by any stretch of the imagination. Once more, I suggest that you utilize IDLE for this present book's activities in case you're simply beginning, except if you are now acquainted with and favor an order line-based improvement mode. There are, be that as it may, a small bunch of elective IDEs for Python designers, some of which are considerably more remarkable and strong than IDLE. Here are the absolute most regularly utilized IDEs:

Eclipse and PyDev: Shroud is a high level open source IDE GUI. Initially created as a Java IDE, Obscuration likewise upholds Python improvement when you introduce the PyDev (or a comparative) module. Overshadowing is a well-known and amazing alternative for Python improvement, and it works out positively past IDLE's list of capabilities. It incorporates support for code culmination, punctuation featuring, linguistic structure investigation, refactoring, troubleshooting, and the sky is the limit from there. Its drawbacks are that it is a huge framework to introduce and may require shareware augmentations for a few highlights (this may fluctuate after some time). In any case, when you are prepared to move on from IDLE, the Eclipse/PyDev mix merits your consideration.

Komodo: A full-highlighted improvement climate GUI for Python (and different dialects), Komodo incorporates standard grammar shading, word processing, investigating, and other highlights. Furthermore, Komodo offers many progressed highlights that IDLE doesn't, counting project documents, source-control reconciliation, ordinary articulation investigating, also, a simplified GUI manufacturer that produces Python/tkinter code to carry out the GUIs you plan intelligently. At this composition, Komodo isn't free.

Net Beans IDE for Python: Net Beans is an amazing open-source improvement climate GUI with help for some high level highlights for Python engineers: code consummation, programmed space and code colorization, editorial manager hints, code collapsing, refactoring, troubleshooting, code inclusion and testing, activities, and then some. It could be utilized to create both CPython and Jython code. Like Eclipse, Net Beans requires establishment ventures past those of the included IDLE GUI, however it is seen by numerous individuals.

Python Win: Python Win is a free Windows just IDE for Python that ships as a feature of Active State's Active Python dissemination. It is generally similar to IDLE, with a modest bunch of helpful Windows explicit augmentations added; for instance, Python Win has support for COM objects. Today, IDLE is presumably further developed than Python Win (for example, IDLE's double interaction design regularly keeps it from hanging). In any case, Python Win actually offers instruments for Windows engineers that IDLE doesn't.

Others: There are generally about six other broadly utilized IDEs that I'm mindful of (counting the business Wing IDE and Python Card) however don't have space to do equity to here, and more will presumably show up over the long run. Truth be told, pretty much every software engineer cordial content tool has a type of help for Python improvement nowadays, regardless of whether it be preinstalled or brought independently. Emacs and Vim, for example, have significant Python support.

I will do whatever it takes not to record all such choices here; for more data, see the assets accessible or scan the Web for "Python IDE." You may likewise take a stab at running a web look for "Python editors" today, this leads you to a wiki page that keeps up data about numerous IDE and word processor choices for Python programming.

1.8 Other Launch Options

Now, we've perceived how to run code composed intelligently, and how to dispatch code saved in documents in an assortment of ways framework order lines, imports and executives, GUIs like IDLE, and the sky is the limit from there. That covers the majority of the cases you'll find in this book. There are extra approaches to run Python code, however, a large portion of which have exceptional or limited jobs. The following not many segments investigate a portion of these.

1.8.1 Embedding Calls

In some particular areas, Python code might be run consequently by an encasing framework. In such cases, we say that the Python programs are inserted in (i.e., run by) another program. The Python code itself might be gone into a book record, put away in an information base, gotten from a HTML page, parsed from a XML report, etc.

Yet, from an operational point of view, another framework not you may advise Python to run the code you've made.

A particularly installed execution mode is usually used to help end-client customization a game program, for example, may consider play changes by running client open inserted Python code at key focuses on schedule. Clients can alter this sort of framework by giving or changing Python code. Since Python code is deciphered, there is no compelling reason to recompile the whole framework to join the change.

In this mode, the encasing framework that runs your code may be written in C, C++, or even Java when the Jython framework is utilized. For instance, it's feasible to make and run strings of Python code from a C program by calling capacities in the Python runtime API (a bunch of administrations sent out by the libraries made when Python is aggregated on your machine).

In this C code piece, a program coded in the C language implants the Python translator by connecting in its libraries, and passes it a Python task proclamation string to run. C projects may likewise access Python modules and articles and measure or execute them utilizing other Python API devices.

This book isn't about Python/C incorporation, yet you ought to know that, depending on how your association intends to utilize Python, you could possibly be the person who as a matter of fact begins the Python programs you make. Notwithstanding, you can generally still utilize the intelligent and document based dispatching strategies depicted here to test code in seclusion from those encasing frameworks that may ultimately utilize it.

1.8.2 Frozen Binary Executable

Frozen twofold executable, are bundles that consolidate your program's byte code and the Python mediator into a solitary executable program. This methodology empowers Python projects to be dispatched in the very manners that you would dispatch some other executable program (symbol clicks, order lines, and so on) While this alternative functions admirably for conveyance of items, it isn't actually proposed for use during program advancement; you ordinarily freeze not long prior to delivery (after improvement is done). See the earlier part for additional on this alternative.

1.8.3 Text Editor Launch Options

As referenced already, despite the fact that they're not out and out IDE GUIs, most developer amicable content tools have support for altering, and potentially running, Python programs. Such help might be inherent or fetch able on the Web. For example, on the off chance that you know about the Emacs word processor, you can do all your Python altering and dispatching from inside that content tool. See the content tool assets page for additional subtleties, or quest the Web for the expression "Python editors."

1.8.4 Still Other Launch Options

Contingent upon your foundation, there might be extra ways that you can begin Python programs. For example, on some Macintosh frameworks you might have the option to drag Python program record symbols onto the Python translator symbol to make them execute, and on Windows you can generally begin Python contents with the Run choice in the Start menu.

Moreover, the Python standard library has utilities that permit Python projects to be begun by other Python programs in discrete cycles, and Python contents may likewise be produced in bigger settings like the Web (for example, a page may summon a content on a worker); nonetheless, these are past the extent of the current section.

1.8.5 Future Possibilities?

This part reflects current practice, yet a large part of the material is both stage and time explicit. For sure, large numbers of the execution and dispatch subtleties introduced emerged during the timeframe of realistic usability of this present book's different versions. Likewise with program execution choices, it's certainly feasible that new program dispatch choices may emerge over the long run.

New working frameworks, and new forms of existing frameworks, may likewise give execution procedures past those laid out here. When all is said in done, in light of the fact that Python stays up with such changes, you ought to have the option to dispatch Python programs in the manner bodes well for the machines you use, both now and later on be that by drawing on tablet PCs or PDAs, snatching symbols in an augmented simulation, or yelling a content's name over your colleagues' discussions.

Execution changes may likewise affect dispatch conspires fairly (e.g., a full compiler could deliver ordinary executable that are dispatched similar as frozen doubles today). In the event that I understood what the future genuinely held, however, I would presumably be conversing with a stockbroker as opposed to composing these words!

1.9 Which Option Should I Use?

With every one of these alternatives, one inquiry normally emerges: which one is best for me? In general, you should check the IDLE interface out on the off chance that you are simply beginning with Python. It gives an easy to use GUI climate and conceals a portion of the fundamental setup subtleties. It additionally accompanies a stage nonpartisan content tool for coding your contents, and it's a norm and free piece of the Python framework.

On the off chance that, then again, you are an accomplished software engineer, you may be more alright with just your preferred content manager in one window, and another window for dispatching the projects you alter by means of framework order lines and symbol clicks (indeed, this is the way I create Python programs, yet I have a Unix-one-sided past). Since the decision of advancement conditions is abstract, I can't offer substantially more in the method of widespread rules; as a rule, whatever climate you like to utilize will be the awesome you to utilize.

1.10 Debugging Python Code

Normally, none of my per users or understudies at any point have bugs in their code (embed smiley here), yet for less blessed companions of yours who may, here's a brief glance at the methodologies usually utilized by genuine Python developers to troubleshoot code:

• Do nothing. By this, I don't imply that Python developers don't troubleshoot their code however when you commit an error in a Python program, you get an exceptionally helpful what's more, comprehensible mistake message (you'll will see some soon, in the event that you haven't as of now).

In the event that you definitely know Python, and particularly for your own code, this is regularly enough read the blunder message, and go fix the labeled line and record. For some, this is troubleshooting in Python. It may not generally be ideal for bigger framework you didn't compose, however.

• Insert print articulations. Likely the principle way that Python developers troubleshoot their code (and the way that I troubleshoot Python code) is to embed print articulations and run once more. Since Python pursues promptly changes, this is normally the fastest approach to get more data than blunder messages give. The print proclamations don't need to be complex a straightforward "I'm here" or show of variable qualities is typically enough to give the setting you need. Simply recall to erase or remark out the troubleshooting prints before you transport your code!

• Use IDE GUI debuggers. For bigger frameworks you didn't compose, and for amateurs who need to follow code in more detail, most Python advancement GUIs have a few kind of point and snap investigating support. Inactive has a debugger as well, however it doesn't have all the earmarks of being utilized frequently by and by maybe in light of the fact that it has no order line, or on the other hand maybe in light of the fact that adding print proclamations is normally faster than setting up a GUI troubleshooting meeting. To find out additional, see IDLE's Help, or just give it a shot your own; its fundamental interface is depicted in the segment "Progressed IDLE Instruments". Other IDEs, like Eclipse, Net Beans, Komodo, and Wing IDE, offer progressed point-and-snap debuggers too; see their documentation on the off chance that you use them.

• Use the pdb order line debugger. For extreme control, Python accompanies a source-code debugger named pdb, accessible as a module in Python's norm library. In pdb, you type orders to step line by line, show factors, set and clear breakpoints, proceed to a breakpoint or mistake, etc. pdb can be dispatched intuitively by bringing in it, or as a high level content. In any case, on the grounds that you can type orders to control the meeting, it gives an amazing troubleshooting instrument. pdb additionally incorporates a posthumous capacity you can pursue.

• Other choices. For more explicit investigating prerequisites, you can discover extra apparatuses in the open source area, including support for multithreaded programs, inserted code, and cycle connection. The Winpdb framework, for instance, is an independent debugger with cutting edge investigating backing and cross-stage GUI what's more, reassure interfaces.

These alternatives will turn out to be more significant as we begin composing bigger contents. Likely the best news on the investigating front, however, is that mistakes are identified and revealed in Python, as opposed to passing quietly or smashing the framework out and out.

Indeed, mistakes themselves are an all-around characterized instrument known as special cases, which you can catch and measure. Committing errors is in no way enjoyable, obviously, yet talking as somebody who reviews while troubleshooting implied getting out a hex number cruncher and poring over heaps of memory dump print outs, Python's investigating support makes mistakes substantially less excruciating than they may in any case be.

Chapter 2. Introducing Python Object Types

This part starts our visit through the Python language. From a casual perspective, in Python, we get things done with stuff. "Things" appear as activities like expansion and link, and "stuff" alludes to the articles on which we play out those tasks. In this piece of the book, our emphasis is on that stuff, and the things our projects can do with it.

To some degree all the more officially, in Python, information appears as articles either implicit objects that Python gives, or items we make utilizing Python or outer language instruments, for example, C expansion libraries. Despite the fact that we'll solidify this definition later, objects are basically bits of memory, with qualities and sets of related activities.

Since objects are the most essential thought in Python programming, we'll start this part with a study of Python's inherent article types. Via presentation, be that as it may, we should initially build up a reasonable image of how this part finds a way into the general Python picture. From a more solid viewpoint, Python projects can be decayed into modules, proclamations, articulations, and articles, as follows:

1. Projects are made out of modules.

2. Modules contain proclamations.

3. Proclamations contain articulations.

4. Articulations make and cycle objects.

The conversation of modules presented the most elevated level of this progressive system. This present part's sections start at the base, investigating both underlying articles and the articulations you can code to utilize them.

2.1 Why Use Built in Types?

In the event that you've utilized lower-level dialects like C or C++, you realize that a lot of your work fixates on executing objects otherwise called information constructions to address the segments in your application's space. You need to spread out memory structures, oversee memory allotment, execute search and access schedules, etc. These tasks are comparably monotonous (and mistake inclined) as they sound, and they generally divert from your program's genuine objectives.

In normal Python programs, the vast majority of this snort work disappears. Since Python gives incredible article types as a natural piece of the language, there's normally no compelling reason to code object executions before you begin taking care of issues. Indeed, except if you have a requirement for uncommon preparing that underlying sorts don't give, you're quite often good utilizing an inherent item as opposed to executing your own. Here are a few reasons why:

• Built-in objects make programs simple to compose. For straightforward assignments, underlying sorts are frequently all you need to address the construction of issue spaces. Since you get useful assets like assortments (records) and search tables (word references) for nothing, you can utilize them right away. You can complete a ton of work Python's implicit article types alone.

• Built-in objects are parts of expansions. For more intricate assignments, you may have to give your own articles utilizing Python classes or C language interfaces. Be that as it may, as you'll see in later pieces of this book, objects executed physically are regularly based on top of underlying sorts like records and word references. For example, a stack information design might be carried out as a class that oversees or redoes an implicit rundown.

• Built-in objects are frequently more proficient than custom information structures. Python's inherent kinds utilize as of now upgraded information structure calculations that are executed in C for speed. In spite of the fact that you can compose comparative article types on your own, you'll for the most part be unable to get the degree of execution worked in object types give.

• Built in objects are a standard piece of the language. Python acquires both from dialects that depend on worked in apparatuses (e.g., LISP) and dialects that depend on the software engineer to give device executions or structures of their own (e.g., C++). In spite of the fact that you can execute interesting item types in Python, you don't have to do so to begin. Also, in light of the fact that Python's constructed are standard, they're generally something very similar; restrictive systems, then again, will in general vary from one site to another.

At the end of the day, not exclusively do worked in object types make programming simpler, but at the same time they're more impressive and productive than the greater part of what can be made without any preparation. Whether or not you execute new article types, underlying items structure the center of each Python program.

2.1.1 Python's Core Data Types

Python's underlying article types and a portion of the language structure used to code their literals that is, the articulations that produce these items.

A portion of these kinds will presumably appear to be natural in the event that you've utilized different dialects; for example, numbers and strings address numeric and text based qualities, individually, and records give an interface to preparing documents put away on your PC.

Since all that we cycle in Python programs is a sort of article. For example, when we perform text design coordinating in Python, we make design objects, and when we perform network scripting, we use attachment objects.

These different sorts of articles are by and large made by bringing in and utilizing modules and have conduct all their own.

As we'll see in later pieces of the book, program units like capacities, modules, and classes are objects in Python too they are made with proclamations and articulations for example, class, import, and lambda and might be passed around contents openly, put away inside different articles, etc. Python likewise gives a bunch of execution related sorts, for example, arranged code objects, which are by and large important to device manufacturers more than application designers; these are additionally examined in later pieces of this content.

We ordinarily call the other item types as center information types, however, in light of the fact that they are adequately incorporated into the Python language that is, there is explicit articulation punctuation for producing a large portion of them. For example, when you run the accompanying code.

You are, actually talking, running an exacting articulation that creates and returns another string object. There is explicit Python language punctuation to make this item. Additionally, an articulation enclosed by square sections makes a rundown, one in wavy supports makes a word reference, etc. Despite the fact that, as we'll see, there are no sort presentations in Python, the punctuation of the articulations you run decides the kinds of items you make and use. Indeed, object-age articulations like those are for the most part where types begin in the Python language.

Similarly as significantly, when you make an item, you tie its activity set forever you can perform just string procedure on a string and rundown procedure on a rundown. As you'll learn, Python is powerfully composed (it monitors types for you consequently as opposed to requiring affirmation code), however it is likewise specifically (you can perform on an item just tasks that are substantial for its sort).

Practically, the item types are more broad and amazing than what you might be acclimated with. For example, you'll see that rundowns and word references alone are amazing information portrayal devices that hinder the greater part of the work you do to help assortments and looking in lower-level dialects. So, records give requested assortments of different articles, while word references store objects by key; the two records and word references might be settled, can develop and recoil on request, and may contain objects of any sort.

We'll concentrate every one of the item types in detail in forthcoming sections. Prior to diving into the subtleties, however, how about we start by investigating Python's center articles in real life. The remainder of this section gives a review of the tasks we'll investigate in more profundity in the parts that follow. Try not to hope to track down the full story here the objective of this section is simply to spark your interest and present some key thoughts. All things considered, the most ideal approach to begin is to begin, so we should hop directly into some genuine code.

2.2 Numbers

In the event that you've done any programming or scripting previously, a portion of the item types will most likely appear to be recognizable. Regardless of whether you haven't, numbers are genuinely straight forward. Python's center items set incorporates the standard suspects: whole (numbers without a fragmentary part), coasting point numbers (generally, numbers with a decimal point in them), and more extraordinary numeric sorts (complex numbers with nonexistent parts, fixed accuracy decimals, sane portions with numerator and denominator, and full included sets).

Despite the fact that it offers some fancier alternatives, Python's essential number sorts are, all things considered, fundamental. Numbers in Python support the typical numerical activities. For example, the additionally sign performs option, a star is utilized for increase, and two stars are utilized for exponentiation.

Notice the last outcome here: Python whole number sort naturally gives additional accuracy to huge numbers like this when required (in 2.6, a different long number sort handles numbers excessively huge for the typical whole number sort comparably). You can, for example, process 2 to the force 1,000,000 as a whole number in Python

The principal result isn't a bug; it's a showcase issue. Incidentally, there are two different ways to print each item: with full accuracy (as in the main outcome appeared here), and in an easy to use structure (as in the second). Officially, the main structure is referred to as an item's as code, and the second is it's easy to use. The distinction can matter when we venture up to utilizing classes; for the time being, if something looks odd, take a stab at showing it with a print inherent call articulation.

Python additionally incorporates more outlandish numeric items like mind boggling, fixed-accuracy, furthermore, normal numbers, just as sets and Booleans and the outsider open source expansion area has significantly more (e.g., grids and vectors). We'll concede conversation of these kinds until some other time in the book.

Up until this point, we've been utilizing Python similar as a basic number cruncher; to improve equity to its underlying kinds, how about we proceed onward to investigate strings.

2.3 Strings

Strings are utilized to record literary data just as discretionary assortments of bytes. They are our first illustration of what we call a succession in Python that is, a positional requested assortment of different articles. Arrangements keep a left-to-correct request among the things they contain: their things are put away and gotten by their relative position. Stringently talking, strings are arrangements of one-character strings; different kinds of groupings incorporate records and tuples, covered later.

2.3.1 Sequence Operations

As groupings, strings support tasks that expect a positional requesting among things. For instance, in the event that we have a four-character string, we can check its length with the implicit capacity and bring its segments with ordering articulations.

In Python, lists are coded as balances from the front, thus start from 0: the principal thing is at file 0, the second is at list 1, etc.

Notice how we dole out the string to a variable named S here. We'll broadly expound on how this functions later, however Python factors never should be proclaimed early. A variable is made when you allocate it a worth, might be appointed any kind of article, and is supplanted with its worth when it appears in an articulation. It should likewise have been recently appointed when you utilize its worth. For the reasons for this part, it's sufficient to realize that we need to appoint an item to a variable to save it for some time in the future.

Notice that we can utilize a discretionary articulation in the square sections, not simply a hard coded number exacting anyplace that Python anticipates a worth, we can utilize a strict, a variable, or any articulation. Python's linguistic structure is totally broad thusly.

Notwithstanding basic positional ordering, arrangements likewise support a more broad type of ordering known as cutting, which is an approach to remove a whole segment (cut) in a solitary advance.

Likely the most straightforward approach to consider cuts is that they are an approach to remove a whole section from a string in a solitary advance. Their overall structure, X signifies "give me everything in X from counterbalance I up to yet excluding balance J." The outcome is returned in another item. The second of the first tasks, for example, gives us every one of the characters in string S from counterbalances 1 through 2 (that is, 3 − 1) as another string. The impact is to cut or "parse out" the two characters in the center.

Note how negative counterbalances can be utilized to give limits for cuts, as well, and how the last activity adequately duplicates the whole string. As you'll learn later, there is no motivation to duplicate a string, yet this structure can be valuable for groupings like records.

At long last, as groupings, strings additionally support connection with the in addition to sign (joining two strings into another string) and reiteration (making another string by rehashing another).

Notice that the in addition to sign (+) implies various things for various items: expansion for numbers, and link for strings. This is an overall property of Python that we'll call polymorphism later in the book in whole, the significance of an activity relies upon the articles being worked on. As you'll see when we study dynamic composing, this polymorphism property represents a significant part of the brevity and adaptability of Python code.

Since types aren't obliged, a Python-coded activity can typically chip away at various kinds of articles consequently, as long as they support a viable interface (like the + activity here). This ends up being an enormous thought in Python; you'll study it later on our visit.

2.3.2 Immutability

Notice that in the earlier models, we were not changing the first string with any of the activities we ran on it. Each string activity is characterized to deliver another string as its outcome, since strings are permanent in Python they can't be changed set up after they are made. For instance, you can't change a string by allocating to one of its positions, however you can generally construct another one and dole out it to a similar name. Since Python tidies up old articles as you go (as you'll see later), this isn't just about as wasteful as it might sound.

Each item in Python is delegated either permanent (unchangeable) or not. Regarding the center kinds, numbers, strings, and tuples are unchanging; records and word references are not (they can be changed set up openly). In addition to other things, unchanging nature can be utilized to ensure that an article stays consistent all through your program.

2.3.3 Type Specific Methods

Each string activity we've concentrated so far is actually a grouping activity that is, these tasks will deal with different arrangements in Python also, including records and tuples. Notwithstanding conventional arrangement activities, however, strings likewise have tasks all their own, accessible as strategies capacities joined to the item, which are set off with a call articulation.

For instance, the string discover technique is the essential substring search activity (it returns the balance of the passed-in substring in the event that it is absent), and the string supplant strategy performs worldwide pursuits and substitutions.

Once more, in spite of the names of these string techniques, we are not changing the first strings here, yet making new strings as the outcomes since strings are unchanging, we need to do it thusly. String techniques are the principal line of text-preparing apparatuses in Python. Different techniques split a string into substrings on a delimiter (helpful as a basic type of parsing), perform case transformations, test the substance of the string (digits, letters, etc.), and strip whitespace characters off the finishes of the string.

One note here: in spite of the fact that arrangement activities are conventional, strategies are not albeit a few sorts share some technique names, string strategy tasks for the most part work just on strings, and that's it. As a dependable guideline, Python's toolset is layered: nonexclusive activities that range various sorts appear as inherent capacities or articulations, however type-explicit tasks are strategy calls. Discovering the devices you need among every one of these classes will turn out to be more normal as you use Python more, yet the following area gives a couple of tips you can utilize at this moment.

2.3.4 Getting Help

The techniques presented in the earlier segment are an agent, yet little, example of what is accessible for string objects. As a rule, this book isn't comprehensive in its glance at object strategies. For additional subtleties, you can generally call the worked in work, which returns a rundown of the multitude of properties accessible for a given article. Since strategies are work ascribes, they will appear in this rundown. Accepting S is as yet the string, here are its credits on Python.

You presumably will not think often about the names with underscores in this rundown until some other time in the book, when we study administrator over-burdening in classes they address the execution of the string object and are accessible to help customization. By and large, driving and following twofold underscores is the naming example Python utilizes for execution subtleties. The names without the underscores in this rundown are the callable techniques on string objects.

Help is one of a small bunch of interfaces to an arrangement of code that ships with Python known as PyDoc a device for extricating documentation from objects. Later in the book, you'll see that PyDoc can likewise deliver its reports in HTML design.

You can likewise request help on a whole string (e.g., help(S)), however you may get more assistance than you need to see i.e., data about each string strategy. It's by and large better to get some information about a particular technique.

For additional subtleties, you can likewise counsel Python's standard library instructional booklet or monetarily distributed reference books, however help are the main line of documentation in Python.

2.3.5 Other Ways to Code Strings

Up until now, we've taken a gander at the string article's grouping activities and type-explicit strategies. Python likewise gives an assortment of approaches to us to code strings, which we'll investigate in more prominent profundity later. For example, uncommon characters can be addressed as oblique punctuation line get away from groupings.

Python permits strings to be encased in single or twofold statement characters (they mean exactly the same thing). It likewise permits multiline string literals encased in triple statements (single or twofold) when this structure is utilized, every one of the lines are connected together, and end of-line characters are added where line breaks show up. This is a minor syntactic comfort, yet it's valuable for inserting things like HTML and XML code in a Python content.

Python additionally upholds a crude string exacting that turns off the oblique punctuation line get away from system (such string literals start with the letter r), just as Unicode string support that upholds internationalization. In latest version, the fundamental string type handles Unicode as well (which bodes well, given that ASCII text is a straightforward sort of Unicode), and a bytes type addresses crude byte strings; in older version, Unicode is a different kind, and handles both 8-bit strings and twofold information. Records are likewise changed in latest version to return and acknowledge text and bytes for parallel information. We'll meet every one of these extraordinary string structures in later sections.

2.3.6 Pattern Matching

One point important before we proceed onward is that none of the string item's techniques support design based content handling. Text design coordinating is a high level apparatus outside this present book's extension, however per users with foundations in other scripting dialects might be intrigued to realize that to do design coordinating in Python, we import a module.

This model looks for a substring that starts with "Hi," trailed by at least zero tabs or spaces, trailed by subjective characters to be saved as a coordinated with bunch, ended by "world." If such a substring is discovered, segments of the substring coordinated by parts of the example encased in enclosures are accessible as gatherings. The accompanying example, for instance, selects three gatherings isolated by cuts.

Example coordinating is a genuinely progressed text-handling device without anyone else, yet there is moreover support in Python for much further developed language handling, including regular language preparing. I've effectively said enough regarding strings for this instructional exercise, however, so how about we proceed onward to the following kind.

2.4 Lists

The Python list object is the broadest succession given by the language. Records are positional requested assortments of discretionarily composed articles, and they have no fixed size. They are likewise changeable not at all like strings, records can be altered set up by task to balances just as an assortment of rundown strategy calls.

2.4.1 Sequence Operations

Since they are groupings, records support all the succession activities we talked about for strings; the solitary contrast is that the outcomes are typically records rather than strings. For example, given a three thing list.

2.4.2 Type Specific Operations

Python's rundowns are identified with clusters in different dialects, yet they will in general be all the more remarkable. For a certain something, they have no fixed sort limitation the rundown we just took a gander at, for instance, contains three objects of totally various sorts (a whole number, a string, and a skimming point number). Further, records have no fixed size. That is, they can develop and contract on request, because of rundown explicit activities.

Here, the rundown affix technique grows the rundown's size and embeds a thing toward the end; the pop strategy (or an identical explanation) at that point eliminates a thing at a given counterbalance, making the rundown contract. Other rundown strategies embed a thing at a self-assertive position (embed), eliminate a given thing by esteem (eliminate, etc. Since records are variable, most rundown strategies additionally change the rundown object set up, rather than making another one.

2.4.3 Bounds Checking

In spite of the fact that rundowns have no fixed size, Python actually doesn't permit us to reference things that are absent. Ordering off the finish of a rundown is consistently an error, however so is doling out off the end.

This is deliberate, as it's normally a mistake to attempt to allot off the finish of a rundown (and a especially dreadful one in the C language, which doesn't do as much blunder checking as Python). Maybe than quietly developing the rundown accordingly, Python reports a blunder. To grow a rundown, we call list strategies, for example, attach all things considered.

2.4.4 Nesting

One pleasant element of Python's center information types is that they support self-assertive settling we can settle them in any blend, and as profoundly as we like (for instance, we can have a rundown that contains a word reference, which contains another rundown, etc.). One prompt utilization of this element is to address networks, or "multidimensional exhibits" in Python. A rundown with settled records will do the work for essential applications.

The primary activity here brings the whole second line, and the second gets the third thing inside that line. Hanging together file activities takes us more profound and more profound into our settled item structure.

2.4.5 Comprehensions

Notwithstanding grouping activities and rundown techniques, Python incorporates a further developed activity known as a rundown cognizance articulation, which ends up being an incredible method to handle structures like our framework. Assume, for example, that we need to separate the second section of our example lattice. It's not difficult to get columns by straightforward ordering.

This network structure works for limited scope assignments, however for more genuine calculating you will likely need to utilize one of the numeric augmentations to Python, for example, the open source NumPy framework. Such instruments can store and deal with enormous networks considerably more productively than our settled rundown structure. NumPy has been said to transform Python into what might be compared to a free and all the more impressive adaptation of the Matlab framework, and associations, for example, NASA, Los Alamos, and JPMorgan Chase utilize this apparatus for logical and monetary undertakings. Quest the Web for additional subtleties.

Rundown appreciations get from set documentation; they are an approach to construct another rundown by running an articulation on everything in a grouping, each in turn, from left to right. Rundown appreciations are coded in square sections (to warn you to the way that they make a rundown) and are made out of an articulation and a circling build that share a variable name (line, here). The former rundown perception implies essentially what it says: "Give me row for each line in grid M, in another rundown." The outcome is another rundown containing section 2 of the lattice.

The principal activity here, for example, adds 1 to everything as it is gathered, and the second uses if proviso to sift odd numbers through of the outcome utilizing the % modulus articulation (rest of division). Rundown appreciations make new arrangements of results, yet they can be utilized to emphasize over any item. Here, for example, we use list perceptions to venture over a hardcoded rundown of directions and a string.

Rundown appreciations, and family members like the guide and channel worked in capacities, are a piece excessively included for me to say really regarding them here. The central matter of this short acquaintance is with delineate that Python remembers both straightforward and progressed apparatuses for its arms stockpile. Rundown appreciations are a discretionary element, yet they will in general be helpful practically speaking and regularly give a generous preparing speed advantage. They additionally work on any kind that is a grouping in Python, just as certain sorts that are definitely not. You'll hear substantially more about them later in this book.

As a review, however, you'll see that in ongoing Pythons, understanding linguistic structure in brackets can likewise be utilized to make generators that produce results on request (the aggregate implicit, for example, entireties things in an arrangement).

2.5 Dictionaries

Python word references are something totally extraordinary (Monty Python reference proposed) they are not successions by any means, however are rather known as mappings.

Mappings are additionally assortments of different items, yet they store objects by key rather than by relative position. Truth be told, mappings don't keep up any dependable left-to-correct request; they basically map keys to related qualities. Word references, the solitary planning type in Python's center articles set, are likewise variable: they might be changed set up and can develop and contract on request, similar to records.

2.5.1 Mapping Operations

At the point when composed as literals, word references are coded in wavy supports and comprise of an arrangement of "key: esteem" sets. Word references are helpful whenever we need to connect a bunch of qualities with keys to depict the properties of something, for example. For instance, think about the accompanying three-thing word reference (with keys "food," "amount," and "shading").

We can list this word reference by key to bring and change the keys' related qualities. The word reference record activity utilizes the very language structure as that utilized for arrangements, yet the thing in the square sections is a key, not a relative position.

Albeit the wavy supports strict structure sees use, it is maybe more normal to see word references developed in an unexpected way. The accompanying code, for instance, begins with an unfilled word reference and rounds it out each key in turn. Not at all like beyond the field of play tasks in records, which are prohibited, have tasks to new word had reference keys made those keys.

Here, we're successfully utilizing word reference keys as field names in a record that portrays somebody. In different applications, word references can likewise be utilized to supplant looking tasks ordering a word reference by key is regularly the quickest method to code a hunt in Python.

2.5.2 Nesting Revisited

In the earlier model, we utilized a word reference to depict a theoretical individual, with three keys. Assume, however, that the data is more mind boggling. Maybe we need to record a first name and a last name, alongside different occupation titles. This prompts another use of Python's item settling in real life. The accompanying word reference, coded at the same time as an exacting, catches more organized data.

Here, we again have a three-key word reference at the top (keys "name," "work," and "age"), in any case, the qualities have gotten more unpredictable: a settled word reference for the name to help numerous parts, and a settled rundown for the task to help different jobs and future development. We can get to the parts of this design much as we accomplished for our network before, however this time a portion of our records are word reference keys, not rundown counterbalances.

Notice how the last activity here extends the settled occupation list on the grounds that the work list is a different piece of memory from the word reference that contains it, it can develop and recoil uninhibitedly (object memory format will be talked about additional later in this book).

The genuine justification showing you this model is to exhibit the adaptability of Python's center information types. As should be obvious, settling permits us to develop complex data structures straightforwardly and without any problem. Building a comparative design in a low-level language like C would be drawn-out and require considerably more code: we would need to spread out and announce constructions and exhibits, round out qualities, interface everything together, etc. In Python, this is all programmed running the articulation makes the whole settled article structure for us. Indeed, this is one of the principle advantages of scripting dialects like Python.

Similarly as critically, in a lower-level language we would need to be mindful so as to tidy up the entirety of the item's space when we at this point don't require it. In Python, when we lose the last reference to the article by appointing its variable to something different, for instance the entirety of the memory space involved by that item's design is consequently tidied up for us.

Actually speaking, Python has an element known as trash assortment that tidies up unused memory as your program runs and liberates you from overseeing such subtleties in your code. In Python, the space is recovered promptly, when the last reference to an item is eliminated. We'll concentrate how this functions later in this book; for the present, it's sufficient to realize that you can utilize protests uninhibitedly, without agonizing over making their space or tidying up as you go.

Remember that the rec record we just made truly could be an information base record, when we utilize Python's item diligence framework a simple method to store local Python objects in documents or access-by-key data sets. We will not go into subtleties here, however watch for conversation of Python's pickle and hold modules later in this book.

2.5.3 Sorting Keys: for Loops

As mappings, as we've effectively seen, word references just help getting to things by key. In any case, they likewise support type-explicit activities with technique calls that are helpful in an assortment of regular use cases.

As referenced before, in light of the fact that word references are not arrangements, they don't keep up any trustworthy left-to-correct request. This implies that in the event that we make a word reference and print it back, its keys may return an unexpected request in comparison to that wherein we composed them.

What do we do, however, in the event that we do have to force a requesting on a word reference's things?

One regular arrangement is to snatch a rundown of keys with the word reference keys strategy, sort that with the rundown sort technique, and afterward venture through the outcome with a Python for circle (make certain to press the Enter key twice in the wake of coding the for circle underneath as clarified), an unfilled line signifies "go" at the intuitive brief, and the brief changes on certain interfaces).

This is a three-venture measure, in spite of the fact that, as we'll see in later sections, in late forms of Python it tends to be done in one stage with the more up to date arranged inherent capacity. The arranged consider returns the outcome and sorts an assortment of article types, for this situation arranging word reference keys naturally.

Other than displaying word references, this utilization case serves to present the Python for circle. The circle is a basic and productive approach to venture through every one of the things in a succession and run a square of code for everything thus. A client characterized circle variable (key, here) is utilized to reference the current thing each time through. The net impact in our model is to print the unordered word reference's keys and qualities, in arranged key request.

The circle, and its more broad cousin the while circle, are the primary ways we code dreary assignments as articulations in our contents. Truly, however, the circle (like its overall the rundown appreciation, which we met prior) is an arrangement activity. It deals with any article that is an arrangement and, similar to the rundown cognizance, even on certain things that are definitely not. Here, for instance, it is venturing across the characters in a string, printing the capitalized adaptation of each as it goes.

2.5.4 Iteration and Optimization

In the event that the last area's for circle resembles the rundown appreciation articulation presented prior, it ought to: both are truly broad emphasis instruments. Indeed, both will deal with any object that follows the emphasis convention an unavoidable thought in Python that basically implies a truly put away grouping in memory, or an article that creates each thing in turn with regards to an emphasis activity. An item falls into the last class on the off chance that it reacts to worked in with an article that propels because of next. The generator understanding articulation we saw before is such an article.

I'll have more to say about the emphasis convention later in this book. For the present, keep in mind that each Python device that examines an article from left to right uses the emphasis convention. This is the reason the arranged call utilized in the earlier area chips away at the word reference straightforwardly we don't need to call the keys strategy to get an arrangement since word references are objects, with a next that profits progressive keys.

The rundown appreciation, however, and related practical programming apparatuses like guide what's more, channel, will commonly run quicker than a for circle today (maybe even twice as fast)a property that could matter in your projects for enormous informational collections. Having said that, however, I should bring up that exhibition measures are interesting business in Python since it advances so a lot, and execution can shift from one delivery to another.

A significant dependable guideline in Python is to code for effortlessness and intelligibility first and stress over execution later, after your program is working, and after you've demonstrated that there is a certifiable presentation concern. As a general rule, your code will be speedy enough for what it's worth. In the event that you do have to change code for execution, however, Python incorporates instruments to take care of you, including the time and time it modules and the profile module. You'll discover more on these later in this book, and in the Python manuals.

2.5.5 Missing Keys: if Tests

One other note about word references before we proceed onward. In spite of the fact that we can allot to another key to grow a word reference, bringing a nonexistent key is as yet a mix up. This is the thing that we need it's typically a programming blunder to get something that isn't truly there. In any case, in some nonexclusive projects, we can't generally understand what keys will be present when we compose our code. How would we deal with such cases and keep away from mistakes? One stunt is to test early. The word reference in enrollment articulation permits us to inquiry the presence of a key and branch on the outcome with a Python if proclamation (similarly as with for, make certain to press Enter twice to run if intuitively here).

I'll have substantially more to say about the if proclamation and explanation punctuation in everyday later in this book, yet the structure we're utilizing here is direct: it comprises of the word if, trailed by an articulation that is deciphered as a valid or bogus outcome, trailed by a square of code to run if the test is valid. In its full structure, if articulation can likewise have an else proviso for a default case, and at least one (else if) provisos for different tests.

It's the primary choice device in Python, and it's the manner in which we code rationale in our contents.

All things considered, there are alternate approaches to make word references and try not to get to nonexistent keys: the get technique (a restrictive file with a default); the Python has key strategy (which is not, at this point accessible); the attempt articulation (an instrument we'll initially meet that gets and recuperates from exemptions out and out); and the if/else articulation (basically, an if explanation pressed onto a solitary line).

2.6 Tuples

The tuple object is generally like a rundown that can't be changed tuples are successions, similar to records, however they are unchanging, similar to strings. Linguistically, they are coded in enclosures rather than square sections, and they support subjective sorts, discretionary settling, and the typical succession activities.

2.6.1 Why Tuples?

Anyway, why have a sort that resembles a rundown, however upholds less activities? To be honest, tuples are not for the most part utilized as regularly as records by and by, yet their changelessness is the entirety point. In the event that you pass an assortment of items around your program as a rundown, it very well may be changed anyplace; in the event that you utilize a tuple, it can't. That is, tuples give such a respectability requirement that is advantageous in programs bigger than those we'll compose here. We'll speak more about tuples later in the book. Until further notice, however, we should get out ahead to our last significant center sort: the document.

2.7 Files

Record objects are Python code's primary interface to outside documents on your PC. Documents are a center sort, however they're something of a weirdo there is no particular strict language structure for making them. Maybe, to make a document object, you call the implicit open capacity, passing in an outer filename and a handling mode as strings. For instance, to make a book yield record, you would pass in its name and the 'w' preparing mode string to compose information.

This makes a record in the current index and composes text to it (the filename can be a full catalog way in the event that you need to get to a record somewhere else on your PC). To peruse back what you just composed, resume the record in 'r' handling mode, for understanding content input this is the default on the off chance that you discard the mode in the call. At that point read the record's substance into a string, and show it. A document's substance are consistently a string in your content, paying little heed to the sort of information the record contains.

Other record object strategies support extra highlights we don't have the opportunity to cover here. For example, document objects give more methods of perusing and composing (read acknowledges a discretionary byte size, read line peruses each line in turn, etc.), just as different apparatuses (look for moves to another record position). As we'll see later, however, the most ideal approach to peruse a document today is to not peruse it at all records give an iterator that naturally peruses line by line in for circles and different settings.

We'll meet the full arrangement of document strategies later in this book, yet on the off chance that you need a fast see currently, run an approach any open record and an assistance on any of the strategy names that return.

Later in the book, we'll additionally see that documents in Python draw a sharp qualification among text and parallel information. Text records address content as strings and perform Unicode encoding and interpreting naturally, while parallel documents address content as an uncommon bytes string type and permit you to get to record content unaltered.

Despite the fact that you will not for the most part need to think often about this differentiation in the event that you manage ASCII text, Python strings and records are a resource on the off chance that you manage internationalized applications or byte arranged information.

2.7.1 Other File like Tools

The open capacity is the workhorse for most document handling you will do in Python. For further developed assignments, however, Python accompanies extra record like devices: pipes, FIFOs, attachments, keyed-access documents, constant item retires, descriptor based records, social and article arranged information base interfaces, and the sky is the limit from there. Descriptor records, for case, support document locking and other low level devices, and attachments give an interface to systems administration and bury measure correspondence. We will not cover a large number of these subjects in this book, however you'll see them helpful once you begin programming Python decisively.

2.8 Other Core Types

Past the center sorts we've seen up until this point, there are others that might fit the bill for enrollment in the set, contingent upon how comprehensively it is characterized. Sets, for instance, are a new expansion to the language that are neither mappings nor successions; rather, they are unordered assortments of novel and changeless articles. Sets are made by calling the implicit set capacity or utilizing new set literals and articulations, and they support the typical numerical set tasks (the decision of new language structure for set literals bodes well, since sets are similar as the keys of a worthless word reference).

Furthermore, Python as of late grew a couple of new numeric sorts: decimal numbers (fixed accuracy skimming point numbers) and division numbers (judicious numbers with both a numerator and a denominator). Both can be utilized to work around the restrictions and intrinsic errors of gliding point math.

Python additionally accompanies Booleans (with predefined True and False articles that are basically the whole numbers 1 and 0 with custom presentation rationale), and it has since a long time ago upheld an extraordinary placeholder object called None normally used to introduce names and items.

2.8.1 How to Break Your Code's Flexibility

I'll have more to say pretty much the entirety of Python's article types later, however one benefits extraordinary treatment here. The sort object, returned by the kind underlying capacity, is an article that gives the kind of another item; its outcome contrasts marginally, in light of the fact that types have converged with classes totally (something we'll investigate with regards to "new style" classes). Expecting L is as yet the rundown of the earlier area.

Other than permitting you to investigate your articles intelligently, the viable use of this is that it permits code to check the kinds of the items it measures. Indeed, there are in any event three different ways to do as such in a Python content.

Since I've shown you every one of these approaches to do type testing, notwithstanding, I am needed by law to reveal to you that doing so is quite often some unacceptable activity in a Python program (and regularly an indication of an ex C software engineer initially beginning to utilize Python!). The motivation behind why will not turn out to be totally clear until some other time in the book, when we begin composing bigger code units like capacities, yet it's a (maybe the) center Python idea. By checking for explicit sorts in your code, you viably break its adaptability you restrict it to chipping away at only one sort. Without such tests, your code might have the option to chip away at an entire scope of types.

This is identified with the possibility of polymorphism referenced before, and it comes from Python's absence of type assertions. As you'll learn, in Python, we code to protest interfaces (tasks upheld), not to types. Not thinking often about explicit sorts implies that code is consequently material to a significant number of them any article with a viable interface will work, paying little mind to its particular kind. Despite the fact that type checking is upheld and surprisingly needed, in some uncommon cases you'll see that it's not typically the "Python" perspective. Truth be told, you'll see that polymorphism is most likely the vital thought behind utilizing Python well.

Conclusion

In this book, we've taken a gander at normal approaches to dispatch Python programs: by running code composed intuitively, and by running code put away in documents with framework order lines, record symbol clicks, module imports, executive calls, and IDE GUIs like IDLE. We've covered a ton of practical startup domain here. This current section's objective was to furnish you with enough data to empower you to begin thinking of some code, which you'll do in the following piece of the book. There, we will begin investigating the Python language itself, starting with its center information types.

In the first place, however, take the typical section test to practice what you've realized here. Since this is the last section in this piece of the book, it's followed with a bunch of more complete activities that test your dominance of this whole part's themes. For assist with the last arrangement of issues, or only for a boost, make certain to go to Appendix B after you've checked the activities out.

LEARN

PYTHON

PROGRAMMING

A COMPLETE GUIDE TO MASTER THE BASICS OF PYTHON PROGRAMMING

BY JOHN BROWN

© Copyright 2021 by - All rights reserved.

This document is geared towards providing exact and reliable information in regards to the topic and issue covered. The publication is sold with the idea that the publisher is not required to render accounting, officially permitted, or otherwise, qualified services. If advice is necessary, legal or professional, a practiced individual in the profession should be ordered.

- From a Declaration of Principles which was accepted and approved equally by a Committee of the American Bar Association and a Committee of Publishers and Associations.

In no way is it legal to reproduce, duplicate, or transmit any part of this document in either electronic means or in printed format. Recording of this publication is strictly prohibited and any storage of this document is not allowed unless with written permission from the publisher. All rights reserved.

The information provided herein is stated to be truthful and consistent, in that any liability, in terms of inattention or otherwise, by any usage or abuse of any policies, processes, or directions contained within is the solitary and utter responsibility of the recipient reader. Under no circumstances will any legal responsibility or blame be held against the publisher for any reparation, damages, or monetary loss due to the information herein, either directly or indirectly.

Respective authors own all copyrights not held by the publisher.

The information herein is offered for informational purposes solely and is universal as such. The presentation of the information is without a contract or any type of guarantee assurance.

The trademarks that are used are without any consent, and the publication of the trademark is without permission or backing by the trademark owner. All trademarks and brands within this book are for clarifying purposes only and are owned by the owners themselves, not affiliated with this document.

Chapter 1. Introduction to Numeric Types in Python

This section starts our top to bottom visit through the Python language. In Python, information takes the type of items either underlying articles that Python gives, or articles we make utilizing Python devices and different dialects like C. Truth be told, objects are the premise of each Python program you will at any point compose. Since they are the most essential idea in Python programming, objects are additionally our first concentration in this book.

In the first section, we took a fast disregard Python's center item types. Albeit fundamental terms were presented around there, we tried not to cover such a large number of particulars in light of a legitimate concern for space. Here, we'll start a more cautious second glance at information type ideas, to fill in subtleties we disregarded before. We should begin by investigating our first information type class: Python's numeric sorts.

1.1 Numeric Type Basics

The greater part of Python's number kinds are genuinely normal and will most likely appear to be natural if you've utilized practically some other programming language previously. They can be utilized to monitor your bank balance, the distance to Mars, the quantity of guests to your site, and pretty much some other numeric amount.

In Python, numbers are not actually a solitary article type, but rather a class of comparable sorts. Python upholds the standard numeric sorts (whole numbers and skimming focuses), just as literals for making numbers and articulations for preparing them. Moreover, Python gives further developed numeric programming backing and articles for further developed work.

A total stock of Python's numeric tool kit incorporates (as shown in Figure 1):

• Integers and coasting point numbers

- Complex numbers
- Fixed exactness decimal numbers
- Rational part numbers
- Sets
- Booleans
- Unlimited whole number accuracy
- An assortment of numeric fabricated and modules

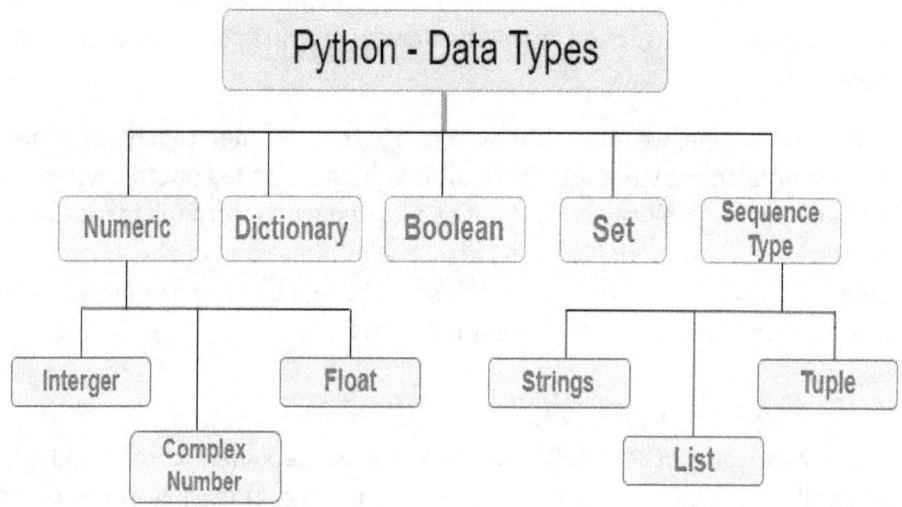

Figure 1: Python Data Types

This section begins with essential numbers and basics, at that point proceeds onward to investigate different apparatuses in this rundown. Before we bounce into code, however, the following not many areas kick us off with a concise outline of how we compose and measure numbers in our contents.

1.1.1 Numeric Literals

Among its essential kinds, Python gives whole numbers (positive and negative entire numbers) and coasting point (numbers with a fragmentary part, here and there called "skims" for economy). Python additionally permits us to compose numbers utilizing hexadecimal, octal, and parallel literals; offers an unpredictable number sort; and permits numbers to have limitless accuracy (they can develop to have however many digits as your memory space permits). Shows what Python's numeric kinds resemble when worked out in a program, as literals.

When all is said in done, Python's numeric sort literals are direct to compose, however a couple of coding ideas merit featuring here:

Integer and floating-point literals

Numbers are composed as strings of decimal digits. Coasting point numbers have a decimal point and additionally a discretionary marked type presented by an e or E and followed by a discretionary sign. In the event that you compose a number with a decimal point or type, Python makes it a drifting point article and uses coasting point (not number) math when the item is utilized in an articulation. Skimming point numbers are carried out as C "copies," and along these lines get as much exactness as the C compiler used to fabricate the Python translator provides for duplicates.

Integers in Python: normal and long

In Python there are two number sorts, typical (32 pieces) and long (limitless accuracy), and a number may end in (I) or (L) to constrain it to turn into a long whole number.

Since numbers are consequently changed over to long whole numbers when their qualities flood 32 pieces, you never need to type the letter L yourself Python consequently changes over up to long number when additional accuracy is required.

Integers in Python: a single type

In Python, the ordinary and long whole number sorts have been converged there is as it were whole number, which consequently upholds the limitless exactness of Python separate long number sort. Along these lines, numbers can at this point don't be coded with a following l or L, and numbers never print with this character all things considered. Aside from this, most projects are unaffected by this change, except if they do type testing that checks for long numbers.

Hexadecimal, octal, and binary literals: Numbers might be coded in decimal (base 10), hexadecimal (base 16), and octal (base 8), or then again paired (base 2). Hexadecimals start with a main 0x or 0X, trailed by a string of hexadecimal digits (0–9 and A–F). Hex digits might be coded in lower-or capitalized. Octal literals start with a main 0o or 0O (zero and lower-or capitalized letter "o"), trailed by a series of digits (0–7). In 2.6 and prior, octal literals can likewise be coded with simply a main 0, yet not in 3.0 (this unique octal structure is too without any problem mistaken for decimal, and is supplanted by the new 0o arrangement). Parallel literals, start with a main 0b or 0B, trailed by twofold digits (0–1).

Note that these literals produce whole number articles in program code; they are simply elective linguistic uses for determining values. The inherent calls hex (I), octal (I), and bin (I) convert a whole number to its portrayal string in these three bases, changes over a runtime string to a number for each a given base.

Complex numbers: Python complex literals are composed as genuine part in addition to fanciful part, where the fanciful part is ended with a j or J. The genuine part is actually discretionary, so the fanciful part may show up all alone. Inside, complex numbers are carried out as sets of gliding point numbers, however all numeric activities perform complex numerical when applied to complex numbers. Complex numbers may likewise be made with the complex (real, picture) worked in call.

Coding other numeric types

As we'll see later in this section, there are extra, further developed number sorts excluded. A portion of these are made by calling capacities in imported modules (e.g., decimals and parts), and others have exacting grammar all their own (e.g., sets).

1.1.2 Built in Numeric Tools

Other than the implicit number literals, Python gives a bunch of apparatuses to preparing number items. We'll meet these as we come.

In spite of the fact that numbers are principally handled with articulations, constructed, and modules, they additionally have a modest bunch of type-explicit strategies today, which we'll meet in this section too. Coasting point numbers, for instance, have an as number proportion strategy that is valuable for the division number sort, and is whole number technique to test if the number is a number. Whole numbers have different ascribes, including another piece length strategy in the forthcoming Python most recent delivery that gives the quantity of pieces important to address the article's worth. Additionally, as part assortment and part number, sets likewise support the two strategies and articulations. Since articulations are the most fundamental device for number sorts, however, how about we go to them next.

1.1.3 Python Expression Operators

Maybe the most basic apparatus that cycles numbers is the articulation: a blend of numbers (or different items) and administrators that registers a worth when executed by Python. In Python, articulations are composed utilizing the standard numerical documentation and administrator images. For example, to add two numbers X and Y you would say X + Y, which advises Python to apply the + administrator to the qualities named by X and Y.

The consequence of the articulation is the amount of X and Y, another number article. Many are clear as crystal; for example, the standard numerical administrators are upheld. A couple of will be natural on the off chance that you've utilized different dialects before: % registers a division leftover portion, plays out a bitwise left-move, and processes a bitwise AND result, etc. Others are more Python-explicit, and not all are numeric in nature: for instance, this is administrator tests object character (i.e., address in memory, an exacting type of equity), and lambda makes anonymous capacities.

Mixed operators follow operator precedence

As in many dialects, in Python, more unpredictable articulations are coded by hanging together the administrator articulations. For example, the amount of two augmentations may be composed as a blend of factors and administrators.

Things being what they are, how does Python know which activity to perform first? The response to this inquiry lies in administrator priority. At the point when you compose an articulation with more than one administrator, Python bunches its parts as per what are called priority rules, and this gathering decides the request wherein the articulation's parts are registered.

It is requested by administrator priority:

• Operators lower in the table have higher priority, thus tie all the more firmly in blended articulations.

• Operators in a similar line by and large gathering from left to right when joined (with the exception of exponentiation, which gatherings option to left, and correlations, which chain left to right).

For instance, assuming you compose Python assesses the augmentation first, adds that outcome to X since it has higher priority than in addition to sign. Essentially, in this present segment's unique model, both augmentation will occur before their outcomes are added.

Parentheses group sub expressions

You can disregard priority totally in the event that you're mindful so as to bunch portions of articulations with enclosures. At the point when you encase sub expressions in enclosures, you supersede Python's priority rules; Python consistently assesses articulations in brackets first prior to utilizing their outcomes in the encasing articulations.

For example, rather than coding you could keep in touch with one of the accompanying to compel Python to assess the articulation in the ideal request.

In the principal case, in addition to sign is applied to X and Y first, since this sub expression is enclosed by brackets. In the subsequent case, it is performed first (similarly as though there were no enclosures by any stretch of the imagination). As a rule, adding brackets in huge articulations is a smart thought it powers the assessment request you need, yet in addition helps lucidness.

Mixed types are converted up

Other than blending administrators in articulations, you can likewise blend numeric sorts. For example, you can add a whole number to a skimming point.

In any case, this prompts another inquiry: what type is the outcome whole number or drifting point? The appropriate response is basic, particularly on the off chance that you've utilized practically some other language previously: in blended sort numeric articulations, Python first proselytes operands up to the kind of the most confounded operand, and afterward plays out the math on same kind operands. This conduct is like sort changes in the C language.

Python positions the intricacy of numeric kinds like so: whole numbers are more straightforward than drifting point numbers, which are easier than complex numbers. Along these lines, when a number is blended in with a skimming point, as in the previous model, the number is changed over up a drifting degree esteem first, and coasting point math yields the gliding point result. Additionally, any blended sort articulation where one operand is an intricate number outcomes in the other operand being changed over up to an unpredictable number, and the articulation yields a mind boggling result. (In Python, typical whole numbers are likewise changed over to long numbers at whatever point their qualities are too huge to even consider fitting in an ordinary number; in most recent form, numbers subsume yearns totally.)

You can compel the issue by calling worked in capacities to change over types physically. Ever, you will not ordinarily need to do this: since Python naturally changes over up to the more unpredictable sort inside an articulation, the outcomes are regularly what you need.

Additionally, remember that all these blended kind changes apply just when blending numeric sorts (e.g., a whole number and a coasting point) in an articulation, including those utilizing numeric and correlation administrators. All in all, Python doesn't change over across some other sort limits naturally. Adding a string to a number, for instance, brings about a blunder, except if you physically convert either; watch for a model when we meet strings in later section.

Operator overloading and polymorphism

In spite of the fact that we're zeroing in on worked in numbers at this moment, all Python administrators might be over burden (i.e., carried out) by Python classes and C expansion types to chip away at objects you make. For example, you'll see later that articles coded with classes might be added or connected with in addition to sign articulations, recorded with articulations, etc.

Besides, Python itself naturally over-burdens a few administrators, to such an extent that they perform various activities relying upon the sort of underlying items being prepared.

For instance, the in addition to sign administrator performs expansion when applied to numbers however performs link when applied to grouping articles like strings and records. Indeed, in addition to sign can mean anything at all when applied to objects you characterize with classes.

As we found in the earlier section, this property is typically considered polymorphism a term demonstrating that the significance of an activity relies upon the kind of the articles being worked on. We'll return to this idea when we investigate capacities in next section, since it turns into a considerably clearer component around there.

1.2 Numbers in Action

On to the code! Most likely the most ideal approach to comprehend numeric items and articulations is to see them in real life, so we should fire up the intuitive order line and attempt some fundamental yet illustrative tasks (see Chapter 3 for pointers in the event that you need assistance beginning an intelligent meeting).

1.2.1 Variables and Basic Expressions

Most importantly, how about we practice some fundamental math. In the accompanying communication, we initially allocate two factors to numbers so we can utilize them later in a bigger articulation.

Factors are essentially names made by you or Python that are utilized to monitor data in your program. We'll say really regarding this in the following part, yet in Python:

- Variables are made when they are first relegated values.

- Variables are supplanted with their qualities when utilized in articulations.

- Variables should be allocated before they can be utilized in articulations.

- Variables allude to objects and are never announced early.

All in all, these tasks cause the factors to spring into reality consequently. I've likewise utilized a remark here. Review that in Python code, text after an imprint and proceeding to the furthest limit of the line is viewed as a remark and is disregarded. Remarks are an approach to compose comprehensible documentation for your code. Since code you type intelligently is transitory, you will not ordinarily compose remarks in this specific situation, yet I've added them to a portion of this current book's guides to help clarify the code.

In the following piece of the book, we'll meet a connected element documentation strings that joins the content of your remarks to objects.

In case you're working along, you don't have to type any of the remark text from all the way to the finish of the line; remarks are just disregarded by Python and not needed pieces of the assertions we're running.

Presently, how about we utilize our new number items in certain articulations. Now, the estimations of are as yet 3 and 4, individually. Factors like these are supplanted with their qualities at whatever point they're utilized inside an articulation, and the articulation results are repeated back quickly when working intelligently.

In fact, the outcomes being repeated back here are tuples of two qualities on the grounds that the lines composed at the brief contain two articulations isolated by commas; that is the reason the outcomes are shown in brackets (more on tuples later). Note that the articulations work in light of the fact that the factors inside them have been doled out qualities. In the event that you utilize an alternate variable that has never been doled out, Python reports a mistake instead of filling in some default esteem.

You don't have to pre declare factors in Python, however they more likely than not been doled out at any rate once before you can utilize them. Practically speaking, this implies you need to introduce counters to zero preceding you can add to them, in state records to an unfilled rundown before you can annex to them, etc.

Here are two somewhat bigger articulations to delineate administrator gathering and more about changes. In the principal articulation, there are no brackets, so Python consequently bunches the parts as per its priority rules since it is lower than in addition to sign, it ties all the more firmly as is assessed first. The outcome is as though the articulation had been coordinated with enclosures as demonstrated in the remark to one side of the code.

Likewise, notice that every one of the numbers are whole numbers in the primary articulation. Thus, Python performs whole number division and expansion and will give an aftereffect of 5, while Python performs genuine division with leftovers and gives the outcome appeared. On the off chance that you need whole number division in this code (more on division in a second).

In the subsequent articulation, brackets are added around the in addition to sign part to drive Python to assess it first. We additionally made one of the operands drifting point by adding a decimal point. Due to the blended kinds, Python changes over the number referred to by a to a gliding point esteem prior to playing out the in addition to sign. On the off chance that every one of the numbers in this articulation were numbers, number division would yield the shortened whole number 0 in Python however the gliding point 0.8 in Python most recent variant.

1.2.2 Numeric Display Formats

Notice that we utilized a print activity in the remainder of the first models. Without the print, you'll see something that may look somewhat odd from the outset.

Full story behind this odd outcome has to do with the limits of coasting point equipment and its failure to precisely address a few qualities in a set number of pieces. Since PC design is definitely past this current book's degree, however, we'll artfulness this by saying that the entirety of the digits in the initially yield are truly there in your PC's coasting point equipment it's simply that you're not acquainted with seeing them. Truth be told, this is truly a showcase issue the intelligent brief's programmed result reverberation shows a larger number of digits than the print explanation. In the event that you would prefer not to see every one of the digits, use print; as the sidebar Display formats" will clarify, you'll get an easy to understand show.

The last three of these articulations utilize string arranging, an apparatus that takes into account design adaptability, which we will investigate in the forthcoming part on strings. Its outcomes are strings that are normally printed to showcases or reports.

Both of these proselyte subjective items to their string portrayals (and the default intuitive reverberation) produces results that look like they were code; (and the print activity) converts to an ordinarily more easy to use design if accessible. A few articles have both for general use, and with additional subtleties. This thought will reemerge when we study the two strings and administrator over-burdening in classes, and you'll discover more on these fabricated in everyday later in the book.

Other than giving print strings to self-assertive articles, the underlying string is additionally the name of the string information type and might be called with an encoding name to decipher a string from a byte string.

1.2.3 Comparisons: Normal and Chained

Up until now, we've been managing standard numeric tasks (expansion and increase), however numbers can likewise measure up. Ordinary correlations work for numbers precisely as you'd expect they analyze the overall sizes of their operands and return a Boolean outcome (which we would ordinarily test in a bigger proclamation).

Notice again how blended sorts are permitted in numeric articulations (just); in the second test here, Python thinks about qualities regarding the more mind boggling type, coast.

Curiously, Python likewise permits us to bind different correlations together to perform range tests. Bind correlations are such a shorthand for bigger Boolean articulations. So, Python allows us to string together size examination tests to code tied correlations, for example, range tests. The articulation, for example, tests whether B is among A and C; it is comparable to the Boolean test yet is simpler on the eyes (and the console).

1.2.4 Division: Classic, Floor, and True

You've perceived how division functions in the past segments, so you should realize that it acts marginally diversely in Python. Indeed, there are really three kinds of division, and two distinctive division administrators, one of which changes in most recent adaptation.

Exemplary and genuine division. In Python, this administrator performs exemplary division, shortening results for whole numbers and saving remnants for drifting point numbers. In Python, it performs genuine division, continually keeping leftovers paying little mind to types.

Floor division. Included Python old rendition and accessible in both Python forms, this administrator consistently shortens fragmentary leftovers down to their floor, paying little mind to types.

Genuine division was added to address the way that the aftereffects of the first exemplary division model are subject to operand types, thus can be hard to expect in a progressively composed language like Python. Exemplary division was eliminated in light of this requirement administrators execute valid and floor division in most recent adaptation.

In aggregate:

• Now consistently performs genuine division, returning a buoy result that incorporates any remaining portion, paying little mind to operand types. It performs floor division, which shortens the rest of profits a number for whole number operands or a buoy if any operand is a buoy.

• The exemplary division, performing shortening whole number division if the two operands are numbers and buoy division (keeping remnants) in any case. It floors division and fills in as it does in most recent adaptation, performing shortening division for whole numbers and floor division for coasts.

Notice that the information sort of the outcome for is as yet reliant on the operand types: if either is a buoy, the outcome is a buoy; else, it is a whole number. Albeit this may appear to be like the sort subordinate conduct in that inspired its adjustment in most recent form, the kind of the return esteem is considerably less basic than contrasts in the return esteem itself. Besides, in light of the fact that it was given to some degree as a retrogressive similarity apparatus for programs that depend on shortening whole number division (and this is more normal than you may expect), it should return numbers for numbers.

Supporting either Python

In spite of the fact that it conduct varies in the two forms, you can in any case uphold the two variants in your code. In the event that your projects rely upon shortening number division, use it in both. On the off chance that your projects require coasting point results with leftovers for whole numbers, use buoy to ensure that one operand is a buoy around when run in more established adaptation.

Floor versus truncation

One nuance: the administrator is by and large alluded to as shortening division, however it's more precise to allude to it as floor division it shortens the outcome down to its floor, which implies the nearest entire number underneath the genuine outcome. The net impact is to adjust down, not stringently shorten, and this issue for negatives. You can see the distinction for yourself with the Python math module (modules should be imported before you can utilize their substance; more on this later).

When running division administrators, you just truly shorten for positive outcomes, since truncation is equivalent to floor; for negatives, it's a story result (truly, they are both floor, however floor is equivalent to truncation for positives).

On the off chance that you truly need truncation paying little mind to sign, you can generally run a buoy division result through math, paying little heed to Python adaptation (additionally see the round worked in for related usefulness).

Why does truncation matter?

Despite the fact that outcomes still can't seem to come in, it's conceivable that the non-shortening conduct in most recent variant may break a critical number of projects. Maybe on account of a C language heritage, numerous developers depend on division truncation for whole numbers and should figure out how to use in such settings all things considered. Watch for a straightforward indivisible number while circle, and a relating exercise toward the finish of Part IV that delineates such a code that might be affected by this change. Additionally stay tuned for additional on the unique from order utilized in this segment; it's talked about further in later part.

1.2.5 Integer Precision

Division may vary marginally across Python discharges, however it's still genuinely standard. Here's something somewhat more outlandish. As referenced before, Python whole numbers support limitless size.

Python has a different sort for long whole numbers, yet it consequently changes any number excessively huge over to store in a typical number to this kind. Subsequently, you don't have to code any exceptional sentence structure to utilize yearns, and the lone way you can tell that you're utilizing more established adaptation aches is that they print with a following "L".

Limitless accuracy whole numbers are an advantageous implicit instrument. For example, you can utilize them to tally the U.S. public obligation in pennies in Python straightforwardly (in the event that you are so disposed, and have sufficient memory on your PC during the current year's spending plan!). They are likewise why we had the option to raise 2 to such huge forces.

Since Python should accomplish additional work to help their all-inclusive accuracy, number math is typically significantly more slow than ordinary when numbers develop enormous. In any case, in the event that you need the exactness, the way that it's worked in for you to utilize will probably exceed its presentation punishment.

1.2.6 Complex Numbers

Albeit less generally utilized than the kinds we've been investigating up to this point, complex numbers are a particular center item type in Python. On the off chance that you understand what they are, you know why they are valuable; if not, consider this part discretionary perusing.

Complex numbers are addressed as two skimming point numbers the genuine and nonexistent parts and are coded by adding a j or J postfix to the fanciful part. We can likewise compose complex numbers with a nonzero genuine part by adding the two sections with more sign. For instance, the perplexing number with a genuine piece of 2 and a fanciful piece of Here are a few instances of complex math at work.

1.2.7 Hexadecimal, Octal, and Binary Notation

The work changes decimal over to octal, hex to hexadecimal, and container to pair. To go the alternate way, the underlying capacity changes a series of digits over to a whole number, and a discretionary second contention allows you to determine the numeric base.

The capacity, which you'll meet later in this book, regards strings like they were Python code. Hence, it has a comparable impact (yet typically runs all the more gradually it as a matter of fact accumulates and runs the string as a piece of a program, and it expects you can believe the wellspring of the string being run; a cunning client could possibly present a string that erases documents on your machine!).

The punctuation in the second of these models produces a mistake. Despite the fact that it is anything but a mistake, be mindful so as not to start a series of digits with a main zero except if you truly mean to code an octal worth. Python will regard it as base 8, which may not fill in as you'd expect is consistently decimal 8, not decimal 10 (in spite of what you could conceivably think!). This, alongside evenness with the hex and twofold structures, is the reason the octal configuration was changed.

Besides, note that these literals can deliver self-assertively long whole numbers. The accompanying, for example, makes a number with hex documentation and afterward shows it first in decimal and afterward in octal and paired with converters.

1.2.8 Bitwise Operations

Other than the ordinary numeric activities (expansion, deduction, etc.), Python upholds a large portion of the numeric articulations accessible in the C language. This incorporates administrators that treat whole numbers as strings of paired pieces. For example, here it is grinding away performing bitwise move and Boolean tasks.

We will not really expound on "piece fidgeting" here. It's upheld in the event that you need it, and it proves to be useful if your Python code should manage things like organization bundles or pressed paired information delivered by a C program. Know, however, that bitwise tasks are regularly not as significant in an undeniable level language, for example, Python as they are in a low-level language like C. As a general guideline, in the event that you end up needing to flip pieces in Python, you should consider which language you're truly coding. By and large, there are frequently better approaches to encode data in Python than bit strings.

1.2.9 Other Built in Numeric Tools

Notwithstanding its center item types, Python additionally gives both implicit capacities and standard library modules for numeric preparing. The abs worked in capacities, for example, figure forces and supreme qualities, individually. The aggregate capacity appeared here deals with an arrangement of numbers, and min and max acknowledge either a succession or individual contentions. There are an assortment of approaches to drop the decimal digits of skimming point numbers. We met truncation and floor before; we can likewise adjust, both mathematically and for show purposes.

As we saw before, the remainder of these produces strings that we would typically print and upholds an assortment of designing choices. As likewise depicted before, the second to last test here will yield in the event that we envelop it by a print call to demand a more easy to use show. The last two lines actually contrast, however round adjusts a coasting point number yet at the same time yields a drifting point number in memory, while string organizing produces a string and doesn't yield an altered number.

Strangely, there are three different ways to figure square roots in Python: utilizing a module work, an articulation, or an underlying capacity (in case you're keen on execution, we will return to these in an activity and its answer for see which runs faster).

Notice that standard library modules, for example, math should be imported, yet inherent capacities like abs and round are consistently accessible without imports. At the end of the day, modules are outer segments, yet implicit capacities live in a suggested namespace that Python consequently searches to discover names utilized in your program. This namespace relates to the module called assembled in Python. There is substantially more about name goal in the capacity and module parts of this book; for the present, when you hear "module," think "import."

The standard library irregular module should be imported too. This module gives instruments to picking an arbitrary gliding point number somewhere in the range of 0 and 1, choosing an irregular number between two numbers, picking a thing at irregular from an arrangement, and then some.

The irregular module can be helpful for rearranging cards in games, picking pictures aimlessly in a slideshow GUI, performing factual recreations, and considerably more. For additional subtleties, see Python's library manual.

1.3 Other Numeric Types

So far in this part, we've been utilizing Python's center numeric sort's number, coasting point, and complex. These will get the job done for the vast majority of the calculating that most developers will at any point need to do. Python accompanies a modest bunch of more extraordinary numeric sorts, however, that merit a brief glance here.

1.3.1 Decimal Type

Python presented another center numeric sort: the decimal item, officially known as Decimal. Linguistically, decimals are made by calling a capacity inside an imported module, as opposed to running a strict articulation. Practically, decimals resemble coasting point numbers, yet they have a fixed number of decimal focuses. Subsequently, decimals are fixed-exactness drifting point esteems.

For instance, with decimals, we can have a skimming point esteem that consistently holds only two decimal digits. Besides, we can determine how to adjust or shorten the additional decimal digits past the article's cutoff. Despite the fact that it by and large causes a little presentation punishment contrasted with the ordinary skimming point type, the decimal kind is appropriate to addressing fixed exactness amounts like amounts of cash and can assist you with accomplishing numeric precision.

The basics

The last point merits elaboration. As you might definitely know, drifting point math is not exactly precise, due to the restricted space used to store esteems. For instance, the accompanying should yield zero, however it doesn't. The outcome is near nothing, yet there are insufficient pieces to be exact here.

Printing the outcome to deliver the easy to use show design doesn't totally help either, on the grounds that the equipment identified with skimming point math is innately restricted as far as precision.

As demonstrated here, we can make decimal articles by calling the Decimal constructor work in the decimal module and passing in strings that have the ideal number of decimal digits for the subsequent item (we can utilize this capacity to change over skimming guide esteems toward strings if necessary). At the point when decimals of various accuracy are blended in articulations, Python changes over up to the biggest number of decimal digits consequently.

Setting precision globally

Different instruments in the decimal module can be utilized to set the accuracy of every decimal number, set up mistake taking care of, and that's just the beginning. For example, a setting object in this module takes into account determining exactness (number of decimal digits) and adjusting modes (down, roof, and so on) the accuracy is applied all around the world for all decimals made in the calling string.

This is particularly valuable for money related applications, where pennies are addressed as two decimal digits. Decimals are basically an option in contrast to manual adjusting and string arranging in this unique circumstance.

Decimal context manager

Despite the fact that helpful, this assertion requires considerably more foundation information than you've gotten now; watch for inclusion of the proclamation.

Since utilization of the decimal sort is still moderately uncommon by and by, I'll concede to Python's standard library manuals and intuitive assistance for additional subtleties. What's more, since decimals address a portion of a similar drifting point precision issues as the part type, how about we proceed onward to the following area to perceive how the two analyze.

1.3.2 Fraction Type

Python debut another numeric sort, Fraction, which carries out a normal number item. It basically keeps both a numerator and a denominator unequivocally, so as to stay away from a portion of the mistakes and impediments of skimming point math.

Portion is such a cousin to the current Decimal fixed-exactness type portrayed in the earlier area, as both can be utilized to control mathematical precision by fixing decimal digits and determining adjusting or truncation strategies. It's likewise utilized in comparable manners like Decimal, Fraction lives in a module; import its constructor and pass in a numerator and a denominator to make one.

Numeric accuracy

Notice that this is not quite the same as drifting point-type math, which is compelled by the fundamental constraints of coasting point equipment. To think about, here are similar tasks run with drifting point items, and notes on their restricted exactness.

This gliding point constraint is particularly clear for values that can't be addressed precisely given their set number of pieces in memory. Both Fraction and Decimal give approaches to get careful outcomes, though at the expense of some speed. For example, in the accompanying model (rehashed from the earlier segment), coasting point numbers don't precisely offer the zero response expected, however both of different kinds do.

Also, portions and decimals both permit more natural and precise outcomes than skimming focuses once in a while can, in an unexpected way (by utilizing levelheaded portrayal and by restricting accuracy).

Conversions and mixed types

To help division changes, gliding point protests currently have a technique that yields their numerator and denominator proportion, parts have a coast strategy, and buoy acknowledges a Fraction as a contention. Follow through the accompanying association to perceive how this works out (in the subsequent test is extraordinary language structure that extends a tuple into singular contentions; more on this when we study work contention passing.

At last, some sort blending is permitted in articulations, however Fraction should here and there be physically proliferated to hold precision. Study the accompanying cooperation to perceive how this functions.

Admonition: in spite of the fact that you can change over from drifting point to division, at times there is an unavoidable accuracy misfortune when you do as such, in light of the fact that the number is wrong in its unique skimming point structure. At the point when required, you can improve on such outcomes by restricting the greatest denominator esteem.

1.3.3 Sets

Python additionally presented another assortment type, the set an unordered assortment of special and unchanging articles that upholds tasks relating to numerical set hypothesis. By definition, a thing shows up just a single time in a set, regardless of how often it is added. All things considered, sets have an assortment of utilizations, particularly in numeric and data set centered work.

Since sets are assortments of different articles, they share some conduct with objects for example, records and word references that are outside the extent of this part. For instance, sets that can develop and recoil on request, and may contain an assortment of article types. As we'll see, a set demonstrations similar as the keys of a useless word reference, however it upholds additional tasks.

Nonetheless, in light of the fact that sets are unordered and don't plan keys to values, they are neither succession nor planning types; they are a sort class unto themselves. Besides, on the grounds that sets are generally numerical in nature (and for some, per users, may appear to be more scholastic and be utilized significantly less frequently than more inescapable articles like word references), we'll investigate the fundamental utility of Python's set items here.

Set basics in Python

There are a couple of approaches to make sets today, contingent upon whether you are utilizing Python. Since this book covers both, we should start with the more established form case, which likewise is accessible (now and then actually needed) in most recent adaptation; we'll refine this for expansions in a second. To make a set item, pass in a grouping or other item to the underlying set capacity.

Sets made this way support the basic numerical set activities with articulation administrators. Note that we can't play out these articulations on plain arrangements we should make sets from them to apply these instruments.

Notwithstanding articulations, the set item gives techniques that compare to these activities and the sky is the limit from there, and that help set changes the set add strategy embeds one thing, update is a set up association, and eliminate erases a thing by esteem (run an approach any set example or the set sort name to see every one of the accessible strategies). Expecting to be x and y are still as they were in the earlier communication.

As compartments, sets can likewise be utilized in tasks, for circles, and rundown perceptions. Since they are unordered, however, they don't uphold grouping activities like ordering and cutting.

For additional subtleties on set tasks, see Python's library instructional booklet or a reference book. Albeit set activities can be coded physically in Python with different kinds, similar to records and word references (and regularly were before), Python's underlying sets utilize proficient calculations and execution strategies to give fast and standard activity.

Set literals in Python

In the event that you think sets are "cool," they as of late turned out to be perceptibly cooler. In Python we can in any case utilize the set underlying to make set items, yet in addition adds another set strict structure, utilizing the wavy supports in the past saved for word references.

This linguistic structure bodes well, given that sets are basically similar to useless word references since they are unordered, exceptional, and changeless, a set's things carry on similar as a word reference's keys. This operational similitude is much seriously striking given that word reference key records are see objects, which backing set like conduct like crossing points and associations.

Indeed, paying little mind to how a set is made, shows it utilizing the new exacting arrangement. The set implicit is as yet needed to make void sets and to construct sets from existing articles (shy of utilizing set understandings, talked about later in this part), yet the new strict is helpful for instating sets of known design.

Immutable constraints and frozen sets

Sets are amazing and adaptable articles, yet they do have one limitation in the two forms that you should remember generally due to their execution, sets can just contain unchanging item types.

Consequently, records and word references can't be installed in sets, yet tuples can in the event that you need to store compound qualities. Tuples think about by their full qualities when utilized in set tasks.

Tuples in a set, for example, may be utilized to address dates, records, IP addresses, etc. (more on tuples later in this piece of the book). Sets themselves are variable as well, thus can't be settled in different sets straightforwardly; on the off chance that you need to store a set inside another set, the frozen set inherent call works actually like set however makes an unchanging set that can't change and along these lines can be inserted in different sets.

Set comprehensions in Python

Notwithstanding literals, presents a set cognizance build; it is comparative in structure to the rundown cognizance we saw in later parts, however is coded in wavy supports rather than square sections and race to make a set rather than a rundown. Set cognizance run a circle and gather the aftereffect of an articulation on every emphasis; a circle variable offers admittance to the current cycle an incentive for use in the assortment articulation. The outcome is another set made by running the code, with all the ordinary set conduct.

In this articulation, the circle is coded on the right, and the assortment articulation is coded on the left. With respect to list appreciations, we get back practically what this articulation says: "Give me another set containing X squared, for each X in a rundown." Comprehensions can likewise repeat across different sorts of items, like strings (the first of the accompanying models represents the appreciation based approach to make a set from a current article).

Since the remainder of the understandings story depends after basic ideas we're not yet set up to address, we'll delay further subtleties until some other time in this book. We'll meet a first cousin, the word reference cognizance, and I'll have considerably more to say pretty much all appreciations (list, set, word reference, and generator) later. As we'll learn later, all perceptions, including sets, support extra grammar not appeared here, including settled circles and if tests, which can be hard to comprehend until you've gotten an opportunity to consider bigger articulations.

Why sets?

Set activities have an assortment of regular uses, some more reasonable than numerical. For instance, since things are put away just a single time in a set, sets can be utilized to sift copies through of different assortments. Basically convert the assortment to a set, and afterward convert it back once more (since they work in the rundown call here).

Sets can likewise be utilized to monitor where you've effectively been while crossing a chart or other cyclic construction. For instance, the transitive module loader and legacy tree listed models we'll concentrate in later sections individually, should monitor things visited to stay away from circles. Despite the fact that recording states visited as keys in a word reference is productive, sets offer an elective that is basically same (and might be pretty much natural, contingent upon who you inquire).

At last, sets are additionally helpful when managing enormous informational indexes (data set inquiry results, for instance) the convergence of two sets contains protests in like manner to both classifications, and the association contains all things in one or the other set. To delineate, here's a somewhat more reasonable illustration of set tasks at work, applied to arrangements of individuals in a speculative organization, utilizing set literals.

You can discover more subtleties on set activities in the Python library manual and a few numerical and social information base hypothesis messages. Likewise stay tuned for recovery of a portion of the set tasks we've seen here, with regards to word reference see objects in Python.

1.3.4 Booleans

Some contend that the Python Boolean sort, bool, is numeric in nature since its two qualities, True and False, are simply redone variants of the numbers 1 and 0 that print themselves in an unexpected way. Albeit that is all most software engineers need to know, we should investigate this sort in somewhat more detail.

All the more officially, Python today has an unequivocal Boolean information type called bool, with the values True and False accessible as new reassigned worked in names. Inside, the names True and False are examples of bool (as shown in Figure 2), which is thus a subclass (in the item situated feeling) of the implicit number sort int. Valid and False carry on precisely like the numbers 1 and 0, then again, actually they have tweaked printing rationale they print themselves as the words True and False, rather than the digits 1 and 0. bool achieves this by rethinking string designs for its two articles.

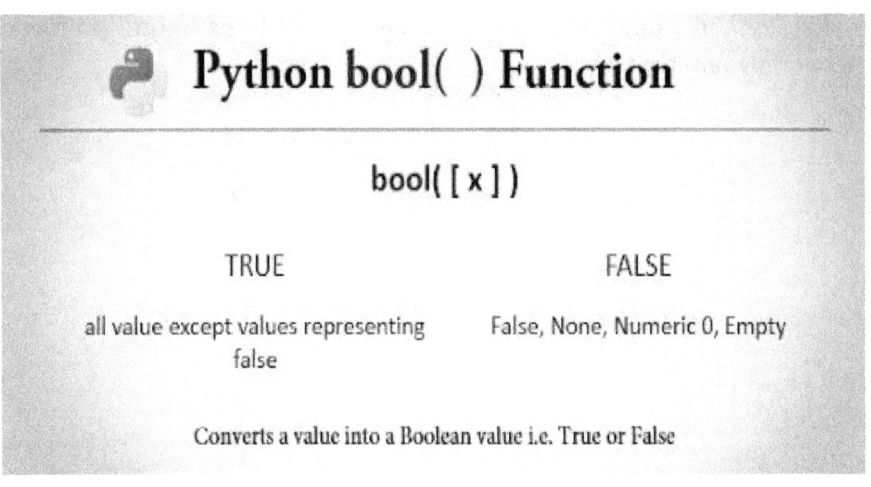

Figure 2: Python bool Function

On account of this customization, the yield of Boolean articulations composed at the intelligent brief prints as the words True and False rather than the more established and more subtle 1 and 0. Moreover, Booleans make truth esteems more unequivocal. For example, a boundless circle would now be able to be coded as while true: rather than the less natural while 1, similarly, banners can be introduced all the more obviously with banner is equivalent to False. We'll talk about these articulations further in Part III.

Once more, however, for any remaining useful purposes, you can regard True and False like they are predefined factors set to whole number 1 and 0. Most software engineers used to reassign True and False to 1 and 0 at any rate; the bool type essentially makes this norm. Its execution can prompt inquisitive outcomes, however. Since True is only the number 1 with a custom presentation design, True in addition to 4 yields 5 in Python. Since you presumably will not go over an articulation like the remainder of these in genuine Python code, you can securely overlook its more profound otherworldly ramifications.

1.4 Numeric Extensions

At long last, in spite of the fact that Python center numeric sorts offer a lot of force for most applications, there is an enormous library of outsider open source expansions accessible to address more centered requirements. Since numeric writing computer programs is a well-known space for Python, you'll discover an abundance of cutting edge apparatuses.

For instance, in the event that you need to do genuine calculating, a discretionary expansion for Python called Numeric Python gives progressed numeric programming instruments, for example, a lattice information type, vector preparing, and modern calculation libraries. Bad-to-the-bone logical programming bunches at places like Los Alamos and NASA use Python with Numeric Python to execute such undertakings they recently coded in C++, FORTRAN, or Matlab. The mix of Python and Numeric Python is regularly contrasted with a free, more adaptable variant of Matlab you get Numeric Python execution, in addition to the Python language and its libraries.

Since it's so exceptional, we will not speak further about Numeric Python in this book. You can discover extra help for cutting edge numeric programming in Python, including designs and plotting apparatuses, measurements libraries, and the mainstream SciPy bundle at Python's PyPI webpage, or via looking through the Web. Likewise note that Numeric Python is presently a discretionary expansion; it doesn't accompany Python and should be introduced independently.

Chapter 2. The Dynamic Typing Interlude

In the earlier section, we started investigating Python's center item types top to bottom with a see Python numbers. We'll continue our item type visit in the following section, yet before we proceed onward, it's significant that you understand what might be the most crucial thought in Python programming and is positively the premise of a lot of both the compactness and adaptability of the Python language dynamic composing, and the polymorphism it yields.

As you'll see here and later in this book, in Python, we don't proclaim the particular kinds of the items our contents use. Indeed, projects ought not to think often about explicit kinds; in return, they are normally material in a greater number of settings than we can now and again even arrangement ahead for. Since dynamic composing is the base of this adaptability, we should investigate the model here.

2.1 The Case of the Missing Declaration Statements

On the off chance that you know quite a bit about aggregated or statically composed dialects like C, C++, or Java, you may wind up somewhat baffled now in the book. Up until now, we've been utilizing factors without proclaiming their reality or their sorts, and it by one way or another works.

When we type any equivalent to 3 of every an intelligent meeting or program document, for example, how does Python realize that should represent a whole number? Besides, how does Python understand what is by any means?

When you begin posing such inquiries, you've gotten over into the space of Python's dynamic composing model. In Python, types are resolved naturally at runtime, not in light of statements in your code. This implies that you never pronounce factors early (an idea that is maybe less difficult to get a handle on in the event that you remember that everything reduces to factors, objects, and the connections between them).

2.1.1 Variables, Objects, and References

As you've seen in a large number of the models utilized so far in this book, when you run an task proclamation like a is equal to 3 in Python, it works regardless of whether you've never told Python to utilize the name an as a variable, or that a should represent a number sort object. In the Python language, this all works out in a characteristic way, as follows:

Variable creation: A variable (i.e., name), like a, is made when your code initially appoints it a worth. Future tasks change the estimation of the all-around made name. In fact, Python identifies a few names before your code runs, however you can consider it however starting tasks make factors.

Variable types: A variable never has any sort data or requirements related with it. The idea of type lives with objects, not names. Factors are conventional in nature; they continuously essentially allude to a specific item at a specific point on schedule.

Variable use: At the point when a variable shows up in an articulation, it is promptly supplanted with the item that it presently alludes to, whatever that might be. Further, all factors should be unequivocally doled out before they can be utilized; referring to unassigned factors results in blunders.

In total, factors are made when allocated, can reference any sort of item, and should be allotted before they are referred to. This implies for instance, should be instated to zero preceding you can add to them. This unique composing model is strikingly not the same as the composing model of customary dialects. At the point when you are initially beginning, the model is generally more obvious in the event that you keep clear the qualification among names and articles. For instance, when we say this.

In any event adroitly, Python will perform three particular strides to do the solicitation. These means mirror the activity of all tasks in the Python language:

1. Make an item to address the worth.

2. Make the variable a, on the off chance that it doesn't yet exist.

3. Connection the variable to the new article.

The net outcome will be a design inside Python that looks like Figure 3. As outlined, factors and items are put away in various pieces of memory and are related by joins (the connection is appeared as a pointer in the Figure 3). Factors consistently connection to items and never to different factors, however bigger articles connection to different items (for example, a rundown object has connections to the items it contains).

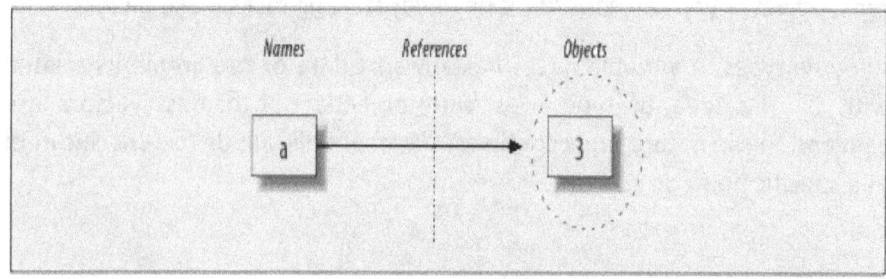

Figure 3: Names and articles after running the task

These connections from factors to objects are called references in Python that is, a reference is a sort of affiliation, executed as a pointer in memory.

At whatever point the factors are subsequently utilized (i.e., referred to), Python consequently follows the variable-to-protest joins. This is all less complex than the wording may suggest. In solid terms:

• Variables are sections in a framework table, with spaces for connections to objects.

• Objects are bits of dispensed memory, with sufficient room to address the qualities for which they stand.

• References are naturally followed pointers from factors to objects.

In any event thoughtfully, each time you produce another worth in your content by running an articulation, Python makes another article (i.e., a lump of memory) to address that esteem. Inside, as a streamlining, Python reserves and reuses particular sorts of unchangeable articles, like little numbers and strings (every 0 isn't actually another piece of memory more on this storing conduct later). In any case, from a coherent point of view, it functions like every articulation's outcome esteem is an unmistakable item and each article is a particular piece of memory.

Actually talking, objects have more design than barely sufficient room to address their qualities. Each item likewise has two standard header handle: a sort designator used to check the kind of the article, and a reference counter used to decide when it's OK to recover the article. To see how these two header fields factor into the model, we need to proceed onward.

2.1.2 Types Live with Objects, Not Variables

To perceive how item types become possibly the most important factor, watch what occurs in the event that we dole out a variable on different occasions.

Per users with a foundation in C may discover Python references like C pointers (memory addresses). Indeed, references are carried out as pointers, and they regularly serve similar jobs, particularly with objects that can be changed set up (additional on this later). Nonetheless, in light of the fact that references are in every case consequently dereferenced when utilized, you can never really do anything helpful with a reference itself; this is a component that kills a huge classification of C bugs. You can consider Python references as C "void" pointers, which are naturally followed at whatever point utilized.

This isn't ordinary Python code, however it tackles job begins as a number, at that point turns into a string, lastly turns into a coasting point number. This model will in general look particularly odd to ex-C software engineers, as it seems like the kind of a progressions from whole number to string when we say an is equivalent to 'spam'.

Notwithstanding, that is not actually what's going on. In Python, things work all the more essentially. Names have no sorts; as expressed prior, types live with objects, not names. In the first posting, we've just changed to reference various articles. Since factors have no sort, we haven't really changed the kind of the variable a; we've just made the variable reference an alternate sort of item. Indeed, again, everything we can at any point say about a variable in Python is that it references a specific article at a specific point on schedule.

Articles, then again, understand what type they are each item contains a header field that labels the article with its sort. The number article 3, for instance, will contain the worth 3, in addition to a designator that discloses to Python that the article is a number (rigorously talking, a pointer to an item, the name of the number kind). The sort designator of the 'spam' string object focuses to the string type all things considered.

Since objects know their sorts, factors don't need to. To recap, types are related with objects in Python, not with factors. In normal code, a given variable generally will reference only one sort of article. Since this isn't a necessity, however, you'll see that Python code will in general be significantly more adaptable than you might be acquainted with on the off chance that you use Python well, your code may chip away at numerous sorts naturally.

I referenced that items have two header handle, a sort designator and a reference counter. To comprehend the last of these, we need to proceed onward and investigate at what occurs toward the finish of an article's life.

2.1.3 Objects Are Garbage Collected

In the earlier segment's postings, we allocated the variable to various kinds of articles in every task. Yet, when we reassign a variable, what befalls the worth it was formerly referring to? For instance, after the accompanying explanations, what befalls the item?

The appropriate response is that in Python, at whatever point a name is allocated to another article, the space held by the earlier item is recovered (in the event that it isn't referred to by some other name or item).

This programmed recovery of items' space is known as trash assortment. To delineate, think about the accompanying model, which sets the name x to an alternate item on every task.

To begin with, notice that x is set to an alternate kind of article each time. Once more, however this is not actually the situation, the impact is like the kind of x is changing over the long run. Keep in mind, in Python types live with objects, not names. Since names are simply conventional references to objects, such a code works normally.

Second, notice that references to objects are disposed of en route. Each time x is relegated to another item, Python recovers the earlier article's space. For example, when it is doled out the string 'growth', the item 42 is quickly recovered (accepting it isn't referred to elsewhere) that is, the article's space is naturally tossed once more into the free space pool, to be reused for a future article.

Inside, Python achieves this accomplishment by keeping a counter in each item that monitors the quantity of references as of now highlighting that object. When (and precisely when) this counter drops to nothing, the article's memory space is naturally recovered. In the first posting, we're accepting that each time x is relegated to another item, the earlier article's reference counter drops to nothing, making it be recovered.

The most quickly substantial advantage of trash assortment is that it implies you can use protests generously while never expecting to let loose space in your content. Python will tidy up unused space for you as your program runs. Practically speaking, this kills a significant measure of accounting code needed in lower level dialects like C and C++.

Actually speaking, Python's trash assortment depends principally upon reference counters, as depicted here; in any case, it likewise has a part that identifies and recovers objects with cyclic references on schedule. This part can be impaired in the event that you're certain that your code doesn't make cycles, yet it is empowered naturally.

Since references are executed as pointers, it's workable for an item to reference itself, or reference another article that does. For instance, practice 3 toward the finish of Part I and its answer in Appendix B tell the best way to make a cycle by implanting a reference to a rundown inside itself.

A similar marvel can happen for tasks to traits of items made from client characterized classes. Despite the fact that moderately uncommon, in light of the fact that the reference means such articles never drop to nothing, they should be dealt with exceptionally.

For additional subtleties on Python's cycle locator, see the documentation for the module in Python's library manual. Additionally note that this depiction of Python's garbage man applies to the standard CPython just; Jython and Iron Python may utilize various plans, however the net impact in everything is comparative unused space is recovered for you naturally.

2.2 Shared References

Up until this point, we've seen what occurs as a solitary variable is allocated references to objects. Presently how about we bring another variable into our association and watch what happens to its names and articles.

Composing these two assertions produces the scene caught in Figure 4. The second line makes Python make the variable b; the variable is being utilized and not appointed here, so it is supplanted with the article it references, and b is made to reference that object. The net impact is that the factors end up referring to a similar article (that is, highlighting a similar lump of memory). This situation, with different names referring to a similar article, is known as a common reference in Python.

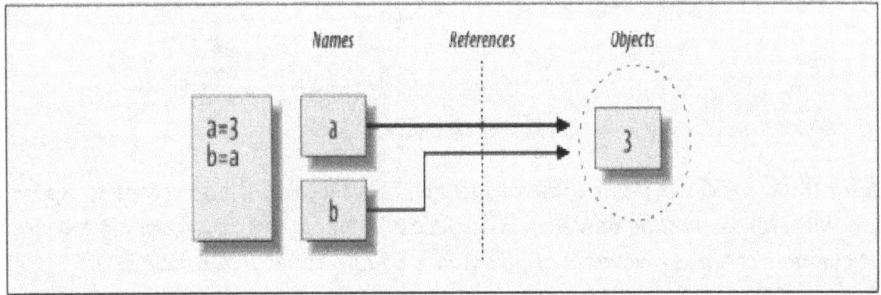

Figure 4: Names and items after next running the task b is equivalent to a. Variable b turns into a reference to the item 3. Inside, the variable is actually a pointer to the article's memory space made by running the exacting articulation 3.

Likewise with all Python tasks, this assertion just makes another item to address the string esteem 'spam' and sets to reference this new article. It doesn't, notwithstanding, change the estimation of b; b actually references the first item, the whole number 3. The subsequent reference structure is appeared in Figure 5.

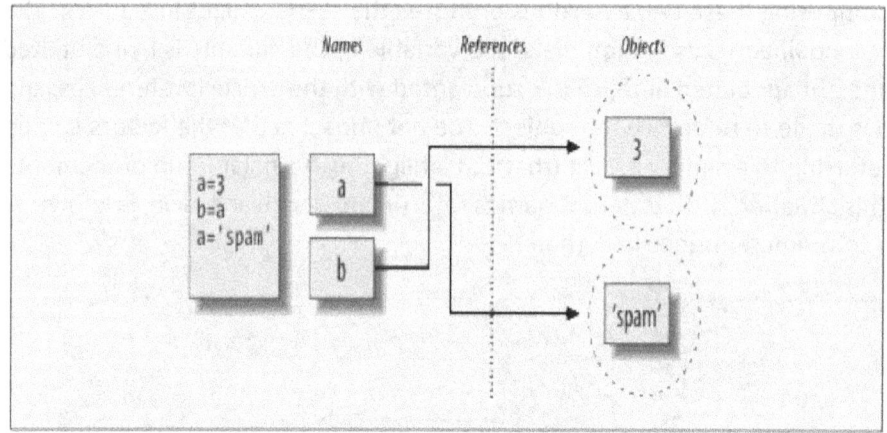

Figure 5: Names and items after at last running the task is equivalent to 'spam'. Variable a references the new item (i.e., piece of memory) made by running the strict articulation 'spam', however factor b actually alludes to the first article 3.

A similar kind of thing would occur on the off chance that we changed b to 'spam' rather the task would change just b, not a. This conduct likewise happens if there are no sort contrasts by any stretch of the imagination.

In this succession, similar situation happen. Python makes the variable a reference the article and makes b reference a similar item as a, as in Figure 4; as in the past, the last task at that point sets a to a totally extraordinary article (for this situation, the whole number, which is the aftereffect of the + articulation). It doesn't change b as a result. Truth be told, it is extremely unlikely to at any point overwrite the estimation of the article, numbers are permanent and consequently can never be changed set up.

One approach to think about this is that, dissimilar to in certain dialects, in Python factors are consistently pointers to objects, not marks of inconsistent memory regions: setting a variable to another worth doesn't modify the first item, but instead purposes the variable to reference a totally unique article. The net impact is that task to a variable can affect just the single variable being appointed. At the point when impermanent items and set up changes enter the condition, however, the image changes to some degree; to perceive how, how about we proceed onward.

2.2.1 Shared References and In Place Changes

As you'll see later in this present part's sections, there are items and activities that act set up object change. For example, a task to a balance in a rundown really changes the rundown object itself set up, as opposed to creating a pristine rundown object.

For objects that help such set up transforms, you should be more mindful of shared references, since a change from one name may affect others.

To additionally show, how about we look again at the rundown objects presented in past section. Review that rundowns, which do uphold set up tasks to positions, are basically assortments of different items, coded in square sections.

L1 here is a rundown containing the items 2, 3, and 4. Things inside a rundown are gotten to by their positions, so L1 alludes to protest 2, the primary thing in the rundown L1. Obviously, records are additionally protests by their own doing, actually like whole numbers and strings. Subsequent to running the two earlier tasks, L1 and L2 reference a similar item, very much like in the earlier model (see Figure 3).

This task just sets L1 is to an alternate article; L2 actually references the first list. On the off chance that we change this present assertion's sentence structure somewhat, in any case, it has a fundamentally unique impact.

Truly, we haven't changed L1 itself here; we've changed a part of the item that L1 references. Such a change overwrites some portion of the rundown object set up. Since the rundown object is shared by (referred to from) different factors, however, a set up change like this doesn't just influence L1 that is, you should know that when you roll out such improvements, they can affect different pieces of your program. In this model, the impact appears in L2 too on the grounds that it references a similar item as L1. Once more, we haven't really changed L2, either, however its worth will seem distinctive in light of the fact that it has been overwritten.

This conduct is typically what you need, yet you ought to know about how it functions, so that it's normal. It's additionally the default: on the off chance that you don't need such conduct, you can demand that Python duplicate articles as opposed to making references. There are an assortment of approaches to duplicate a rundown, remembering utilizing the worked for list work and the standard library duplicate module. Maybe the most widely recognized route is to cut beginning to end.

Here, the change made through L1 isn't reflected in L2 on the grounds that L2 references a duplicate of the article L1 references; that is, the two factors highlight various bits of memory.

Note that this cutting strategy will not work on the other major variable center sorts, word references and sets, since they are not successions to duplicate a word reference or set, utilize their duplicate strategy call. Likewise, note that the standard library duplicate module has a call for replicating any item type conventionally, just as a call for duplicating settled article structures (a word reference with settled records, for instance).

We'll investigate records and word references in more profundity, and return to the idea of shared references and duplicates. Until further notice, remember that protests that can be changed set up (that is, alterable articles) are consistently open to these sorts of impacts.

In Python, this incorporates records, word references, and a few articles characterized with class proclamations. On the off chance that this isn't the ideal conduct, you can basically duplicate your items depending on the situation.

2.2.2 Shared References and Equality

In light of a legitimate concern for complete honesty, I should call attention to that the trash assortment conduct portrayed before in this section might be more calculated than strict for particular sorts.

Since Python stores and reuses little whole numbers and little strings, as referenced prior, the article here is presumably not in a real sense recovered; all things being equal, it will probably stay in a framework table to be reused the following time you create in your code. Most sorts of items, however, are recovered promptly when they are not, at this point referred to; for those that are not, the storing instrument is immaterial to your code.

For example, as a result of Python's reference model, there are two unique approaches to check for correspondence in a Python program.

The primary procedure here, the administrator, tests whether the two referred to objects have similar qualities; this is the technique quite often utilized for fairness checks in Python.

The subsequent technique, the is administrator, rather tests for object character it brings True back just if the two names highlight precisely the same article, so it is a lot more grounded type of fairness testing.

Truly, is basically thinks about the pointers that execute references, and it fills in as a approach to distinguish shared references in your code if necessary. It returns false if the names highlight comparable yet various articles, similar to the situation when we run two distinctive exacting articulations.

In this collaboration, X and Y ought to be (same worth), however not is (same item) on the grounds that we ran two distinctive strict articulations. Since little numbers and strings are stored and reused, however, is reveals to us they reference a similar single article.

Indeed, in the event that you truly need to look in the engine, you can generally ask Python the number of references there are to an item: the get ref include work in the standard sys module returns the article's reference tally. At the point when I get some information about the whole number article 1 in the IDLE GUI, for example, it reports 837 reuses of this equivalent item (the vast majority of which are in IDLE's framework code, not mine).

This article reserving and reuse is unessential to your code (except if you run the check!).

Since you can't change numbers or strings set up, it doesn't make any difference the number of references there are to a similar item. In any case, this conduct reflects one of the numerous ways Python streamlines its model for execution speed.

2.3 Dynamic Typing Is Everywhere

Obviously, you don't actually have to draw name/object charts with circles and bolts to utilize Python. At the point when you're beginning, however, it now and then assists you with understanding surprising cases on the off chance that you can follow their reference structures. In the event that an impermanent item changes free from you when passed around your program, for instance, odds are you are seeing a portion of this present section's topic firsthand.

Besides, regardless of whether dynamic composing appears to be somewhat theoretical now, you most likely will think often about it at last. Since all that appears to work by task and references in Python, an essential comprehension of this model is valuable in a wide range of settings. As you'll see, it works something similar in task articulations, work contentions, for circle factors, module imports, class ascribes, and the sky is the limit from there. Fortunately there is only one task model in Python; when you understand dynamic composing, you'll see that it works a similar wherever in the language.

At the most useful level, unique composing implies there is less code for you to compose. Similarly as critically, however, dynamic composing is additionally the base of Python's polymorphism, an idea we presented in past part and will return to later in this book.

Since we don't compel types in Python code, it is profoundly adaptable. As you'll see, at the point when utilized well, unique composing and the polymorphism it gives produce code that consequently adjusts to new prerequisites as your frameworks advance.

Chapter 3. Strings

The following significant sort on our implicit item visit is the Python string an arranged assortment of characters used to store and address text based data. We took a gander at strings. Here, we will return to them in more profundity, filling in a portion of the subtleties we avoided at that point.

From a utilitarian viewpoint, strings can be utilized to address pretty much whatever can be encoded as text: images and words (e.g., your name), substance of text documents stacked into memory, Internet addresses, Python programs, etc. They can likewise be utilized to hold unquestionably the double estimations of bytes, and multi byte text utilized in internationalized programs.

You may have utilized strings in different dialects, as well. Python's strings serve similar job as character clusters in dialects like C, yet they are a fairly more significant level instrument than exhibits. Not at all like in C, in Python, have strings accompanied an amazing arrangement of preparing instruments. Likewise not at all like dialects, for example, C, Python has no particular kind for singular characters; all things being equal, you simply utilize one character strings.

Stringently speaking, Python strings are classified as unchanging arrangements, implying that the characters they contain have a left-to-right positional request and that they can't be changed set up. Truth be told, strings are the primary agent of the bigger class of items considered successions that we will concentrate here. Give exceptional consideration to the grouping tasks presented in this section, since they will work something very similar on other succession types we'll investigate later, like records and tuples.

Normal string literals and activities we will talk about in this section. Void strings are composed as a couple of quotes (single or twofold) with nothing in the middle, and there are an assortment of approaches to code strings. For handling, strings support articulation activities like link (consolidating strings),

Past the center arrangement of string devices, Python likewise upholds further developed example based string handling with the standard library's re (ordinary articulation) module, presented in past part, and surprisingly more significant level content preparing apparatuses like XML parsers. This present book's extension, however, is centered on the essentials.

To cover the essentials, this section starts with an outline of string exacting structures and string articulations, at that point proceeds onward to see further developed apparatuses like string techniques and organizing. Python accompanies many string instruments, and we will not gander at them all here; the total story is chronicled in the Python library manual. Our objective here is to investigate enough generally utilized devices to give you an agent test; strategies we will not find in real life here, for instance, are to a great extent closely resembling those we will.

In fact talking, this section tells just piece of the string story in Python the part most developers need to know. It presents the essential string type, which handles ASCII text and works a similar paying little mind to which variant of Python you use. That is, this part deliberately restricts its extension to the string handling basics that are utilized in most Python contents.

Python tends to the qualification among text and parallel information by including unmistakable item types:

• In Python there are three string types: string is utilized for text (ASCII or something else), bytes is utilized for double information (counting encoded text), and byte exhibit is a changeable variation of bytes.

• In Python, strings address wide Unicode text, and strings handle both 8 digit text and paired information.

The byte cluster type is likewise accessible as a back port, however not prior, and it's not as firmly bound to double information for what it's worth in most recent variant. Since most developers don't have to delve into the subtleties of encodings or parallel information designs, however, I've moved all such subtleties to the Advanced Topics part of this book.

In the event that you do have to manage further developed string ideas, for example, elective character sets or stuffed double information and records, subsequent to perusing the material here. For the present, we'll center on the fundamental string type and its tasks. As you'll discover, the rudiments we'll concentrate here likewise apply straightforwardly to the further developed string types in Python's instrument set.

3.1 String Literals

All things considered, strings are genuinely simple to use in Python. Maybe the most muddled thing about them is that there are such countless approaches to keep in touch with them in your code.

The single and twofold cited structures are by a wide margin the most well-known; the others serve specific jobs, and we're delaying conversation of the last two progressed structures. We should investigate the wide range of various choices thusly.

3.1.1 Single and Double Quoted Strings Are the Same

Around Python strings, single and twofold statement characters are exchangeable. That is, string literals can be composed encased in either two single or two twofold statements the two structures work something very similar and return a similar sort of item. For instance, the following two strings are indistinguishable, once coded.

The justification supporting both is that it permits you to implant a statement character of the other assortment inside a string without getting away from it with an oblique punctuation line. You may implant a solitary statement character in a string encased in twofold statement characters, and the other way around.

Unexpectedly, Python consequently connects contiguous string literals in any articulation, in spite of the fact that it is nearly as easy to add an or more administrator between them to conjure link unequivocally (as we'll see, enveloping this structure by enclosures likewise permits it to traverse various lines).

Notice that adding commas between these strings would bring about a tuple, not a string. Likewise notice in these yields that Python likes to print strings in single statements, except if they implant one. You can likewise insert cites by getting away from them with oblique punctuation lines.

3.1.2 Escape Sequences Represent Special Bytes

The last model installed a statement inside a string by going before it with an oblique punctuation line.

This is illustrative of an overall example in strings: oblique punctuation lines are utilized to present uncommon byte coding known as break groupings.

Break groupings let us install byte codes in strings that can only with significant effort be composed on a console. The character, and at least one characters following it in the string strict, are supplanted with a solitary character in the subsequent string object, which has the parallel worth determined by the getaway grouping. For instance, here is a five character string that installs a newline and a tab.

The two characters represent a solitary character the byte containing the twofold estimation of the newline character in your character set (ordinarily, ASCII code 10). Essentially, the arrangement is supplanted with the tab character. The manner in which this string looks when printed relies upon how you print it. The intelligent reverberation shows the unique characters as breaks, yet print deciphers them all things considered.

This string is five bytes in length: it contains an ASCII a byte, a newline byte, an ASCII b byte, etc. Note that the first oblique punctuation line characters are not actually put away with the string in memory; they are utilized to advise Python to store exceptional byte esteems in the string. For coding such unique bytes, Python perceives a full arrangement of break code successions.

Some break arrangements permit you to install outright paired qualities into the bytes of a string. For example, here's a five character string that installs two parallel zero bytes (coded as octal breaks of one digit).

In Python, the zero (invalid) byte doesn't end a string the manner in which it normally does in C. All things being equal, Python keeps both the string's length and text in memory. Indeed, no character ends a string in Python. Here's a string that is all outright parallel departure codes a paired 1 and 2 (coded in octal), trailed by a double 3 (coded in hexadecimal).

Notice that Python shows nonprintable characters in hex, paying little mind to how they were indicated. You can unreservedly join supreme worth departures and the more representative getaway types. The accompanying string contains the characters "spam", a tab and newline, and an outright zero worth byte coded in hex.

This turns out to be more imperative to know when you measure double information records in Python. Since their substance are addressed as strings in your contents, it's OK to measure paired records that contain such twofold byte esteems.

In the event that you need to think often about paired information documents, the central differentiation is that you open them in twofold mode. In Python, twofold record content is a bytes string, with an interface like that of ordinary strings, such substance is a typical string. See likewise the standard strict module presented in later part, which can parse twofold information stacked from a document, and the all-encompassing inclusion of double records and byte strings.

Except if you're ready to submit all to memory, however, you presumably shouldn't depend on this conduct. To code strict oblique punctuation lines expressly to such an extent that they are held in your strings, twofold them up or utilize crude strings; the following area shows how.

3.1.3 Raw Strings Suppress Escapes
As we've seen, get away from arrangements are helpful for inserting extraordinary byte codes inside strings. Now and again, however, the exceptional treatment of oblique punctuation lines for acquainting breaks can lead with inconvenience. It's shockingly normal, for example, to see Python new comers in classes attempting to open a document with a filename contention that looks something like this. Feeling that they will open a record called text.dat in the catalog. The issue here is what is taken to represent a newline character, and is supplanted with a tab.

Essentially, the call attempts to open a record named C, with generally not exactly heavenly outcomes. This is only such a thing that crude strings are helpful for. On the off chance that the letter r (capitalized or lowercase) shows up not long before the initial statement of a string, it kills the getaway system. The outcome is that Python holds your oblique punctuation lines in a real sense, precisely as you type them. Subsequently, to fix the filename issue, simply make sure to include the letter Windows.

Likewise with numeric portrayal, the default design at the intelligent brief prints results as though they were code, and consequently escapes oblique punctuation lines in the yield. The print proclamation gives a more easy to use design that shows that there is in reality only one oblique punctuation line in each spot. To confirm this is the situation, you can check the consequence of the inherent length work, which returns the quantity of bytes in the string, autonomous of show designs. On the off chance that you include the characters in the print (way) yield, you'll see that there truly is only 1 character for each oblique punctuation line, for a sum of 15.

Other than catalog ways on Windows, crude strings are additionally generally utilized for ordinary articulations (text design coordinating, upheld with the re module presented in past part). Additionally note that Python contents can as a rule use forward slices in catalog ways on Windows and UNIX since Python attempts to decipher ways transportable. Crude strings are valuable in the event that you code ways utilizing local Windows oblique punctuation lines, however.

Notwithstanding its job, even a crude string can't end in a solitary oblique punctuation line, on the grounds that the oblique punctuation line gets away from the accompanying statement character you actually should get away from the encompassing statement character to install it in the string.

That is certifiably not a substantial string strict a crude string can't end in an odd number of oblique punctuation lines. On the off chance that you need to end a crude string with a solitary oblique punctuation line, you can utilize two and cut off the second, tack one on physically, or avoid the crude string language structure and simply bend over the oblique punctuation lines in an ordinary string. Every one of the three of these structures make a similar eight character string containing three oblique punctuation lines.

3.1.4 Triple Quotes Code Multiline Block Strings

Up until now, you've seen single statements, twofold statements, breaks, and crude strings in real life. Python additionally has a triple-cited string strict arrangement, once in a while called a square string that is a syntactic comfort for coding multiline text information. This structure starts with three statements (of either the single or twofold assortment), is trailed by quite a few lines of text, and is shut with a similar triple-quote succession that opened it. Single and twofold statements inserted in the string's content might be, however don't need to be, got away from the string doesn't end until Python sees three un-got away from statements of a similar kind used to begin the strict.

This string traverses three lines (in certain interfaces, the intuitive brief changes to on continuation lines; IDLE essentially drops down one line). Python gathers all the triple cited text into a solitary multiline string, with inserted newline characters at where your code has line breaks. Notice that, as in the strict, the second line in the outcome has a main space, yet the third doesn't what you type is genuinely what you get. To see the string with the newlines deciphered, print it as opposed to repeating.

Triple cited strings are valuable any time you need multiline text in your program; for model, to insert multiline blunder messages or HTML or XML code in your source code documents. You can insert such squares straightforwardly in your contents without turning to outside text documents or unequivocal link and newline characters.

Triple cited strings are additionally normally utilized for documentation strings, which are string literals that are taken as remarks when they show up at explicit focuses in your record (more on these later in the book). These don't need to be triple-cited blocks, however they ordinarily are to consider multiline remarks.

At last, triple-cited strings are additionally now and again utilized as a "repulsive hacks'" approach to briefly incapacitate lines of code during improvement (OK, it's not actually excessively ghastly, also, it's really a genuinely normal practice). In the event that you wish to kill a couple of lines of code what's more, run your content once more, just put three statements above and underneath them, similar to this.

3.2 Strings in Action

Whenever you've made a string with the exacting articulations we just met, you will nearly positively need to get things done with it. This segment and the following two show string articulations, techniques, and designing the main line of text-preparing apparatuses in the Python language.

3.2.1 Basic Operations

We should start by connecting with the Python translator to show the essential string tasks recorded before. Strings can be connected utilizing the administrator and continued utilizing the administrator.

Officially, adding two string objects makes another string object, with the substance of its operands joined. Redundancy resembles adding a string to itself various occasions. In the two cases, Python allows you to make subjectively estimated strings; there's no compelling reason to pre-declare anything in Python, including the extents of information structures. The length worked in work returns the length of a string (or some other article with a length).

Reiteration may appear to be somewhat dark from the start, yet it proves to be useful in an astounding number of settings. For instance, to print a line of 80 runs, you can tally up to 80, or let Python mean you.

Notice that administrator over-burdening is grinding away here as of now: we're utilizing something similar in addition to sign and administrators that perform expansion and augmentation when utilizing numbers. Python does the right activity since it knows the sorts of the items being added and duplicated. Yet, be cautious: the standards aren't exactly pretty much as liberal as you would anticipate. For example, Python doesn't permit you to blend numbers and strings in addition to sign articulations or rather than consequently changing over to a string.

You can likewise emphasize over strings in circles utilizing for proclamations and test enrollment for the two characters and substrings with the in articulation administrator, which is basically a hunt. For substrings, in is similar as the string discover strategy shrouded later in this part, yet it returns a Boolean outcome rather than the substring's position.

Not at all like with C character clusters, you don't have to apportion or oversee stockpiling exhibits when utilizing Python strings; you can essentially make string objects on a case by case basis and let Python deal with the hidden memory space.

As examined, Python recovers unused articles' memory space consequently, utilizing a reference tally trash assortment procedure. Each article monitors the quantity of names, information structures, and so forth, that reference it; when the check arrives at nothing, Python liberates the item's space. This plan implies Python doesn't need to pause and sweep all the memory to discover unused space to free (an extra trash part moreover gathers cyclic items).

3.2.2 Indexing and Slicing

Since strings are characterized as requested assortments of characters, we can get to their parts by position. In Python, characters in a string are brought by ordering giving the numeric balance of the ideal part in square sections after the string. You get back the one-character string at the predefined position.

As in the C language, Python counterbalances start at 0 and end at one not exactly the length of the string. Dissimilar to C, nonetheless, Python likewise allows you to bring things from successions such as strings utilizing negative counterbalances. Actually, a negative counterbalance is added to the length of a string to determine a positive balance. You can likewise consider negative balances checking in reverse from the end. The accompanying collaboration illustrates.

The primary line characterizes a four-character string and appoints it the name S. The following line records it: gets the thing at balance 0 from the left (the one character strings'), and gets the thing at balance 2 back from the end (or proportionately, at balance from the front). Counterbalances and cuts guide to cells as demonstrated in Figure 6.

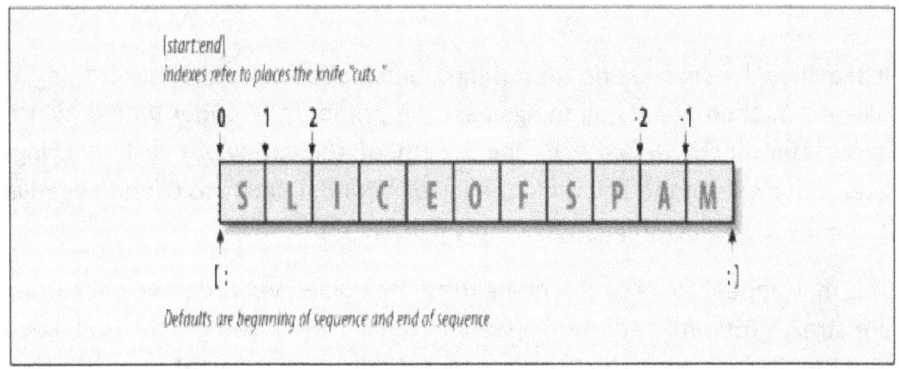

Figure 6: Counterbalances and cuts: positive balances start from the left end (balance 0 is the principal thing), and negatives tally back from the correct end (counterbalance negative 1 is the last thing).

The last line in the former model exhibits cutting, a summed up type of ordering that profits a whole area, not a solitary thing. Likely the most ideal approach to consider cutting is that it is a kind of parsing (dissecting structure), particularly when applied to strings it permits us to extricate a whole area (substring) in a solitary advance. Cuts can be utilized to extricate segments of information, slash off driving and following content, and then some. Truth be told, we'll investigate cutting with regards to message parsing later in this section.

The fundamentals of cutting are direct. At the point when you record an arrangement item like a string on a couple of balances isolated by a colon, Python returns another article containing the touching segment recognized by the counterbalance pair. The left counterbalance is taken to be the lower bound (comprehensive), and the privilege is the upper bound (not comprehensive). That is, Python gets all things from the lower bound up to yet excluding the upper bound, and returns another article containing the got things. Whenever discarded, the left and right limits default to 0 and the length of the article you are cutting, separately.

It snatches the second and third things, and stops before the fourth thing at balance 3. Then, it gets all things past the primary the upper bound, which isn't determined, defaults to the length of the string. At last, it brings everything except the last thing the lower bound defaults to 0, and negative 1 alludes to the last thing, not comprehensive.

This may appear to be confounding from the outset, yet ordering and cutting are straightforward and useful assets to utilize, when you get the skill. Keep in mind, in case you're uncertain about the impacts of a cut, give it a shot intuitively. In the following part, you'll see that it's even conceivable to change a whole segment of another article in one stage by appointing to a cut (however not for permanent like strings).

The last thing recorded here ends up being a typical stunt: it makes a full high level duplicate of an arrangement object an item with a similar worth, yet an unmistakable piece of memory. This isn't exceptionally valuable for permanent articles like strings, yet it proves to be useful for objects that might be changed set up, like records.

In the following part, you'll see that the linguistic structure used to file by counterbalance (square sections) is utilized to file word references by key too; the activities appear to be identical yet have various understandings.

Extended slicing: the third limit and slice objects

In Python, cut articulations have support for a discretionary third record, utilized as a stage (now and again called a step). The progression is added to the list of everything separated. The out and out type of a cut is currently, which signifies "separate all the things in X, from counterbalance I through J, by K." as far as possible, K, defaults to 1, which is why regularly all things in a cut are removed from left to right. On the off chance that you indicate an unequivocal worth, notwithstanding, you can utilize as far as possible to skip things or to invert their request.

For example, X will bring each and every thing from balances 1 to 9; that is, it will gather the things at counterbalances 1, 3, 5, 7, and 9. Of course, the first and second restricts default to 0 and the length of the arrangement, individually, so X gets each and every thing from the start to the furthest limit of the succession.

You can likewise utilize a negative step. For instance, the cutting articulation returns the new string the initial two limits default to 0 and the length of the succession, as in the past, and a step of negative 1 shows that the cut should go from option to left rather than the standard left to right. The impact, thusly, is to turn around the succession.

With a negative step, the implications of the initial two limits are basically turned around. That is, the cut brings the things from 2 to 5, in turn around request (the outcome contains things from balances 5, 4, 3, and 2).

Skipping and switching like this are the most widely recognized use cases for three-limit cuts, be that as it may, see Python's standard library manual for additional subtleties (or run a couple of investigations intelligently). We'll return as far as possible cuts later in this book, related with the for circle proclamation.

Later in the book, we'll additionally discover that cutting is identical to ordering with a cut object, a finding of significance to class essayists looking to help the two activities.

All through this book, I will incorporate regular use case sidebars (like this one) to give you a look at how a portion of the language highlights being presented are regularly utilized in genuine projects. Since you will not have the option to comprehend genuine use cases until you've seen a greater amount of the Python picture, these sidebars essentially contain numerous references to points not presented at this point; probably, you ought to think of them as reviews of ways that you may track down these theoretical language ideas valuable for basic programming undertakings.

For example, you'll see later that the contention words recorded on a framework order line used to dispatch a Python program are made accessible in the property of the worked in sys module.

Ordinarily, you're just keen on examining the contentions that follow the program name. This prompts an extremely normal use of cuts: a solitary cut articulation can be utilized to return everything except the main thing of a rundown. Here, returns the ideal rundown. You would then be able to handle this rundown without obliging the program name at the front.

Cuts are likewise regularly used to tidy up lines read from input records. On the off chance that you realize that a line will have a finish of line character toward the end (newline marker), you can dispose of it with a solitary articulation, for example, line 1, which extricates everything except the last character in the line (as far as possible defaults to 0). In the two cases, cuts do the work of rationale that should be unequivocal in a lower level language.

Note that calling the line technique is regularly liked for stripping newline characters since this consider leaves the line flawless in the event that it has no newline character toward the end a typical case for documents made with some word processing apparatuses. Cutting works in case you're certain the line is appropriately ended.

3.2.3 String Conversion Tools

One of Python's plan proverbs is that it rejects the impulse to figure. As a prime model, you can't gather a number and a string into a single unit in Python, regardless of whether the string resembles a number (i.e., is all digits).

This is by plan: in light of the fact that in addition to sign can mean both expansion and link, the decision of change would be vague. Thus, Python regards this as a mistake. In Python, wizardry is by and large precluded in the event that it will make your life more intricate.

What to do, at that point, if your content gets a number as a book string from a record or client interface? The stunt is that you need to utilize transformation apparatuses before you can deal with a string like a number, or the other way around.

This capacity changes a string over to a number, and the string capacity changes a number over to its string portrayal (basically, what it resembles when printed). The portrayal work (and the more seasoned back quotes articulation, taken out in Python) likewise changes an article over to its string portrayal, yet returns the item as a line of code that can be rerun to reproduce the item. For strings, the outcome has cites around it whenever showed with a print articulation.

Afterward, we'll further investigation the underlying capacity; it runs a string containing Python articulation code thus can change a string over to any sort of article. The capacities and buoy convert just to numbers, yet this limitation implies they are generally quicker (what's more, safer, on the grounds that they don't acknowledge self-assertive articulation code), the string designing articulation likewise gives an approach to change numbers over to strings. We'll talk about arranging further later in this section.

Character code conversions

Regarding the matter of changes, it is likewise conceivable to change a solitary character over to its fundamental ASCII whole number code by passing it to the inherent capacity this profits the real double estimation of the comparing byte in memory. The capacity plays out the opposite activity, taking an ASCII number code and changing it over to the relating character.

You can utilize a circle to apply these capacities to all characters in a string. These apparatuses can likewise be utilized to play out such a string-based math. To progress to the following character, for instance, change over and figure it out in number.

Such changes can be utilized related to circling articulations, and shrouded inside and out in the following piece of this book, to change a line of parallel digits over to their comparing whole number qualities. Each time through the circle, increase the current worth by 2 and add the following digit's number worth.

A left move activity would have a similar impact as increasing by 2 here. We'll leave this change as a recommended work out, however, both on the grounds that we haven't considered circles in detail yet and on the grounds that and canister fabricated ins we met in past part handle twofold transformation assignments for us in Python.

3.2.4 Changing Strings

Recollect the expression "unchanging arrangement"? The unchanging part implies that you can't change a string set up (e.g., by relegating to a list).

Anyway, how would you adjust text data in Python? To change a string, you need to construct and allocate another string utilizing instruments like connection and cutting, and afterward, whenever wanted, appoint the outcome back to the string's unique name.

The main model adds a substring toward the finish of S, by connection (truly, it makes another string and doles out it back to S, and however you can consider this "changing" the first string). The subsequent model replaces four characters with six by cutting, ordering, and linking. As you'll find in the following area, you can accomplish comparable impacts with string strategy calls like supplant.

Like each activity that yields another string esteem, string techniques produce new string objects. In the event that you need to hold those articles, you can appoint them to variable names.

Producing another string object for each string change isn't pretty much as wasteful as it might sound recollect, as examined in the first section, Python naturally trash gathers (recovers the space of) old unused string objects as you go, so more current articles reuse the space held by earlier qualities. Python is generally more effective than you may anticipate.

At last, it's likewise conceivable to develop new content qualities with string organizing articulations. Both of the accompanying substitute items into a string, it could be said changing the articles over to strings and changing the first string as indicated by a configuration detail.

In spite of the replacement similitude, however, the consequence of designing is another string object, not a changed one. We'll examine arranging later in this part; as we'll discover, arranging ends up being more broad and helpful than this model suggests. Since the second of the former calls is given as a technique, however, we should understand string strategy calls before we investigate designing further. Python present another string type known as byte exhibit, which is impermanent thus might be changed set up byte cluster objects aren't actually strings; they're groupings of little,

8 cycle whole numbers. Be that as it may, they support a large portion of similar activities as typical strings and print as ASCII characters when shown. Thusly, they give another choice to a lot of text that should be changed often. We'll additionally see that handle characters which probably won't be put away in single bytes.

3.3 String Methods

Notwithstanding articulation administrators, strings give a bunch of techniques that carry out more refined content preparing assignments. Strategies are essentially works that are related with specific articles. In fact, they are credits joined to objects that end up referring to callable capacities. In Python, articulations and underlying capacities may work across a scope of types, however techniques are by and large explicit to protest types string strategies, for instance, work just on string objects. The technique sets of certain kinds cross in Python (e.g., numerous sorts have a tally strategy), however they are even more sort explicit than different devices.

In better grained detail, capacities are bundles of code, and strategy calls join two tasks on the double (a property get and a call):

Property brings: An outflow of the structure object characteristic signifies "bring the estimation of quality in object."

Call articulations: An outflow of the structure function (arguments) signifies "summon the code of capacity, passing at least zero comma-isolated contention protests to it, and return capacity's outcome esteem."

Assembling these two permits us to call a technique for an article. The strategy call articulation object method (arguments) is assessed from left to right Python will initially bring the strategy for the article and afterward call it, passing in the contentions. On the off chance that the strategy registers an outcome, it will return as the consequence of the whole technique call articulation.

As you'll see all through this piece of the book, most items have callable techniques, and all are gotten to utilizing this equivalent strategy call grammar. To call an article technique, as you'll find in the accompanying segments, you need to go through a current item. These change habitually, so make certain to check Python's standard library manual for the most cutting edge rundown, or run an assistance approach any string intelligently. Python string techniques change marginally; it incorporates decipher, for instance, due to its distinctive treatment of information. In this table, S is a string object, and discretionary contentions are encased in square sections. String strategies in this table execute more significant level tasks like parting and joining, case transformations, content tests, and substring searches and substitutions.

As should be obvious, there are many string techniques, and we don't have space to cover them all; see Python's library manual or reference messages for every one of the fine focuses. To assist you with beginning, however, how about we work through some code that exhibits probably the most normally utilized techniques in real life, and shows Python text-preparing nuts and bolts en route.

Conclusion

This book investigated Python's dynamic composing model that is, the way that Python monitors object types for us consequently, instead of requiring us to code assertion explanations in our contents. En route, we figured out how factors and articles are related by references in Python; we likewise investigated the possibility of trash assortment, figured out what shared references to items can mean for different factors, and perceived what references mean for the idea of fairness in Python.

Since there is only one task model in Python, and in light of the fact that task springs up wherever in the language, it's significant that you have an idea about the model prior to proceeding onward. The accompanying test should help you survey a portion of this current book's thoughts.

CPSIA information can be obtained
at www.ICGtesting.com
Printed in the USA
BVHW090320040521
606332BV00006B/1421